Teaching Success Guide for the Advanced Placement Classroom

The Scarlet Letter

Advanced Placement Classroom

The Scarlet Letter
Advanced Placement Classroom

R. Brigham Lampert

PRUFROCK PRESS INC.
WACO, TEXAS

Library of Congress Cataloging-in-Publication Data

Lampert, R. Brigham.
 The Scarlet Letter / by R. Brigham Lampert.
       pages cm. -- (Teaching Success Guides for the Advanced Placement Classroom)
 Includes bibliographical references.
 ISBN 978-1-61821-031-9 (pbk.)
 1. Hawthorne, Nathaniel, 1804-1864. Scarlet letter. 2. Hawthorne, Nathaniel, 1804-1864--Study and teaching (Higher) I. Title.
 PS1868.L36 2013
 813'.3--dc23
                                 2013005114

Copyright ©2013 Prufrock Press Inc.

Portions of this book were previously published in *Advanced Placement Classroom: Romeo and Juliet* and *Advanced Placement Classroom: King Lear*, also available from Prufrock Press.

Edited by Lacy Compton

ISBN: 978-1-61821-031-9

No part of this book may be reproduced, translated, stored in a retrieval system, or transmitted, in any form or by any means, electronic, mechanical, photocopying, microfilming, recording, or otherwise, without written permission from the publisher.

Prufrock Press grants the individual purchasing this book permission to photocopy original activity pages for single classroom use. This permission does not include electronic reproduction rights. Should you wish to make copies of materials we sourced or licensed from others, request permission from the original publisher before reproducing that material.

For more information about our copyright policy or to request reprint permissions, visit http://www.prufrock.com/permissions.

At the time of this book's publication, all facts and figures cited are the most current available. All telephone numbers, addresses, and website URLs are accurate and active. All publications, organizations, websites, and other resources exist as described in the book, and all have been verified. The author and Prufrock Press Inc. make no warranty or guarantee concerning the information and materials given out by organizations or content found at websites, and we are not responsible for any changes that occur after this book's publication. If you find an error, please contact Prufrock Press Inc.

•AP and Advanced Placement Program are registered trademarks of the College Entrance Examination Board, which was not involved in the production of, and does not endorse, this book.

Prufrock Press Inc.
P.O. Box 8813
Waco, TX 76714-8813
Phone: (800) 998-2208
Fax: (800) 240-0333
http://www.prufrock.com

This book is dedicated to the Jamestown High School class of 2012, a very strong and special group, to many of whom I taught this book.

Contents

Acknowledgements xi

Chapter **1**
Introduction 1

Chapter **2**
Literary Criticism: Ten Ways to See a Book 11

Chapter **3**
Reading *The Scarlet Letter* 39

Chapter **4**
Understanding *The Scarlet Letter* 97

Chapter **5**
Talking About *The Scarlet Letter* 123

Chapter **6**
Writing About *The Scarlet Letter* 143

Resources for Further Study 183
References 187
About the Author 189
Common Core State Standards Alignment 191

Acknowledgments

I am as always grateful to my family, especially my wife, Jennifer, and my parents, the Rev. Dr. Richard and Molly Lampert. I also must express thanks for the College of William and Mary, to which I find myself consistently indebted, and particularly to my former mentor there, Dr. Joyce VanTassel-Baska. This time around, I also wish to express strong gratitude to Prufrock Press and my editor, Lacy Compton, whose extreme patience with my production of this work is greatly and duly appreciated.

Chapter 1

Introduction

In designing and writing this book, I have intended to produce a very user-friendly pedagogical resource for classroom teachers who wish to optimize their students' literary experience and expand their successes, in the honors, pre-AP, and/or Advanced Placement classroom and, more summatively, on the AP English Literature examination. The activities and assignments in this book are targeted for an audience of gifted and talented students, but are moreover appropriate for nongifted learners, including homeschooled pupils. Regardless, I have assumed in writing that the material's intended population is one able to thrive in a rigorous course of study such as that offered—and demanded—by an AP English Literature course. Please note, however, that the material included in this text does not constitute an official College Board curriculum, nor is it officially endorsed by the College Board. It is meant as a curricular supplement for use in Advanced Placement, pre-AP, International Baccalaureate, honors, gifted, and other similarly rigorous advanced English and literature courses.

Bases in Scholarship and Standards

I have fortunately had over my career as a classroom educator numerous opportunities to write contractually and publish educational curricula on a variety of topics and literary works. This professional curricular work began more than a decade ago at the Center for Gifted Education at the College of William and Mary, in Williamsburg, VA. Over several years, I designed, for six different Shakespearean plays, *Navigator* teachers' guides, all based on the Center's—and particularly its director and my former academic advisor, Dr. Joyce VanTassel-Baska's (1986)—Integrated Curriculum Model (ICM), which I once again utilized and emphasized while editing and coauthoring three more comprehensive, yearlong language arts curricula, including *Threads of Change in 19th Century American Literature*, which is in some ways a precursor to this *The Scarlet Letter* text. The same curricular model proved instrumental during my composition of *Advanced Placement Classroom: Romeo and Juliet* and *Advanced Placement Classroom: King Lear*, both of which are also available from Prufrock Press. Needless to say, I am a firm believer in the framework's utility.

Emphasizing academic traditionalism, the ICM is designed to provide gifted and talented students with (a) advanced content knowledge of a given educational discipline or subject, (b) occasions to employ higher order thinking and processing skills while acquiring and utilizing or reinforcing that content knowledge, and (c) considerations of major issues, themes, or ideas that are centrally or peripherally relevant to the studied content, but also important in the world beyond academia, in more than strictly scholastic ways. These three aims or portions of the ICM—the advanced content dimension, the process-product dimension, and the issues/themes dimension, respectively—constitute the didactic structure upon which I designed many of the individual activities in this book, as well as its full pedagogical scope.

Furthermore, I have designed the contents of this text to correlate with national standards for English language arts instruction at the secondary level, in both a general sense and more particular significance to AP Literature and Composition classes. I have therefore utilized two other pedagogical compasses, the first of which is the Standards for the English Language Arts developed by the National Council of Teachers of English (NCTE) and the International Reading Association (IRA; 1996). Table 1 demonstrates the ways in which activities and assignments located within the five major chapters of this book correlate with the NCTE/IRA 12 standards.

Additionally, I have intended to create a useable and useful resource for teachers of *The Scarlet Letter* in actual pre-AP and AP courses, so the second pedagogical guide that I utilized was the College Board's (2007) AP English Literature and Composition Course Description, a document that outlines expectations and recommendations for AP English Literature teachers, students, and syllabi nationwide. This course description does not numerate instructional standards, as the NCTE does, but it does propose and support many specific goals and values for AP-level (i.e., college-level) instruction, according to which I have furthermore designed my activities and assignments, as demonstrated in Table 2.

It is crucial to acknowledge that the AP English Literature and Composition Course Description lists three separate elements that are intrinsic to the close reading and study of a work of literature: (a) the experience of literature, (b) the

TABLE 1

Alignment of Activities and Assignments With the 12 Standards for the English Language Arts Proposed by the National Council of Teachers of English

	Alignment With NCTE Standards for the English Language Arts				
Standard	Chapter 2: Literary Criticism: Ten Ways to See a Book	Chapter 3: Reading The Scarlet Letter	Chapter 4: Understanding The Scarlet Letter	Chapter 5: Talking About The Scarlet Letter	Chapter 6: Writing About The Scarlet Letter
1. Read a wide range of texts for both intrapersonal and societal/cultural understanding, for the acquirement of new information, for response to society's needs, and for personal fulfillment.	✗	✗	✗	✗	✗
2. Read a wide range of literature to build an understanding of the universal human condition.	✗	✗	✗	✗	✗
3. Apply various active linguistic strategies to comprehend, interpret, evaluate, and appreciate texts.	✗	✗	✗	✗	✗
4. Adjust spoken, written, and visual language methods to communicate effectively with various audiences for different purposes.	✗			✗	✗
5. Employ a wide range of writing strategies and elements to communicate effectively with different audiences for various purposes.			✗		✗
6. Apply knowledge of language structure, conventions, techniques, figurative elements, and genre to create, critique, and discuss texts.	✗	✗	✗	✗	✗
7. Conduct self-directed investigative research by gathering, evaluating, and synthesizing data from a variety of sources, then communicate their findings to an audience.			✗	✗	✗
8. Use various technological and information resources to gather and synthesize information and to create and communicate knowledge.		✗	✗	✗	✗
9. Develop an understanding of and respect for diversity in human language use.	✗	✗	✗	✗	✗
10. Non-native English speakers use their first languages to develop competency and understanding in the English language arts and curricula.					
11. Participate as knowledgeable, reflective, creative, and critical members of a variety of literacy communities.	✗	✗	✗	✗	✗
12. Use spoken, written, and visual language to accomplish a variety of their own purposes.	✗	✗	✗	✗	✗

TABLE 2

Alignment of Activities and Assignments With Goals and Curricular Requirements, Both Stated and Implied, Adapted From the College Board's AP English Literature and Composition Course Description

	Alignment With AP English Literature and Composition Goals/Curricular Requirements					
Goal/Requirement	Chapter 2: Literary Criticism: Ten Ways to See a Book	Chapter 3: Reading The Scarlet Letter	Chapter 4: Understanding The Scarlet Letter	Chapter 5: Talking About The Scarlet Letter	Chapter 6: Writing About The Scarlet Letter
1. Intensive study of representative works by canonical Western authors from various time periods, engendering careful, deliberative reading and multiple interpretations.	✗	✗	✗	✗	✗
2. Interpretive, textually based analysis that considers a work of literature's structure, styles, and themes.	✗	✗	✗	✗	✗
3. Interpretive, textually based analysis that considers the social and historical values that a work of literature reflects and embodies.	✗	✗	✗	✗	✗
4. Interpretive, textually based analysis that considers a work of literature's use of such elements as figurative language, imagery, symbolism, and tone.	✗	✗	✗	✗	✗
5. Opportunities to develop understanding of a work of literature, enabling students to discover what they think about their reading via informal, exploratory analytical activities.	✗	✗	✗	✗	✗
6. Opportunities to explain a work of literature via expository analyses that utilize textual details to develop and support interpretations of a text's meaning.	✗	✗	✗	✗	✗
7. Opportunities to evaluate a work of literature's artistry and quality, and its social and cultural values, via argumentative analyses that draw upon textual details.	✗	✗	✗	✗	✗
8. Instruction and feedback that help students develop a wide-ranging vocabulary used appropriately and effectively.	✗	✗	✗	✗	✗
9. Instruction and feedback that help students develop a variety of sentence structures, including appropriate use of subordination and coordination, in their writing.		✗			✗
10. Instruction and feedback that help students develop logical, coherent organization in analysis and writing, including specific techniques such as repetition, transitions, and emphasis.		✗			✗
11. Instruction and feedback that help students develop a balance of generalization and specific, illustrative detail in their analysis.	✗	✗	✗	✗	✗
12. Instruction and feedback that help students develop an effective use of rhetoric in writing and analysis, including such features as tone, voice, and appropriate emphasis in diction and syntax.				✗	✗

interpretation of literature, and (c) the evaluation of literature. The College Board emphasizes these three elements in encouraging particular approaches to designing reading and writing activities, and I have thus done likewise in designing this book's chapters, plans, and activities. These three elements should be considered distinct from, yet naturally imbedded within, the numerated curricular goals and requirements outlined in Table 2.

Additionally, many teachers and states' departments of education are increasingly emphasizing that lessons have accordance to the Common Core State Standards (CCSS). By their natures, all of the activities in this text align with the CCSS for English Language Arts. As a case in point, consider the reformative genesis of the CCSS movement; Vicky Giouroukakis and Maureen Connolly (2012) wrote that "a consistent theme in school reform is the idea that our schools are failing because the standards are too low" (p. 7). Clearly this theme is inconsistent with the rigorous standards of AP courses, which, of course, aim to replicate college-level instruction and thoroughness, as do the activities in this book. As Silver, Dewing, and Perini (2012) explained, "If we could distill the Common Core State Standards into one overarching theme, it would likely be 'Develop students' higher-order and critical thinking skills'" (p. 50). Such development is the central premise of this text and my pedagogical approach to its design.

Moreover, all of the reading standards of the CCSS "are aligned with the National Assessment of Educational Progress (NAEP) assessment framework in reading," Giouroukakis and Connolly (2012) noted, and "reading standard 10 [specifically] requires the reading of high-quality texts in a range of genres of increasing complexity," into which categories both *The Scarlet Letter* itself and its "The Custom-House" introductory chapter fall. An overarching emphasis of the CCSS is "the vital role of evidence in supportive thinking," which is similarly a backbone of many of the exercises, assignments, and activities in this text (Silver et al., 2012, p. 7). Also, "the writing standards [in particular] consist of three different types of writing: argument, explanatory, and narrative (standards 1–3)" (Giouroukakis & Connolly, 2012, p. 8). *Advanced Placement Classroom: The Scarlet Letter* allows students opportunities to engage in and practice all three of these compositional forms.

Silver and colleagues (2012) further explained that "to become college and career ready, students must have ample opportunities to take part in a variety of rich, structured conversations—as part of a whole class, in small groups, and with a partner—built around content" (p. 37). This book is rife with such opportunities, particularly as set forth in Chapter 5: Talking About *The Scarlet Letter*, but moreover by the nature of the questions that it poses throughout its assessments, assignments, and activities; as Carol Jago (2011) clarified, "probing questions [such as those utilized in Advanced Placement Classroom: *The Scarlet Letter*] point the way to important or puzzling lines, introducing areas of debate and inviting diverse interpretations," thereby engendering the higher-order cognitive practice and skills inherent to the CCSS (p. 10). Overall, therefore, this book's design and contents invite you to aid your students not only in preparing for the AP English Literature examination, but also in developing and utilizing those skills and techniques that are at the forefront of modern American educational reform. "In short," the Common Core State Standards Initiative (http://corestandards.org) itself explained in 2012, "students who meet the standards develop the skills in reading, writing, speaking, and listening that are the foundation for any creative and purposeful expression in language" (para. 6); opportunities for developing these skills are found throughout the pages of this particular text.

Organization of This Text

This book includes five chapters of approaches, activities, and exercises to augment your classroom instruction of *The Scarlet Letter*. Surely I recognize that to utilize all of the materials contained within these five chapters would probably take more than the time that most classroom teachers allot for a unit study of one literary work, even a novel as complex and fertile as *The Scarlet Letter*. However, I personally believe it better to be overplanned than underplanned, and I thus provide an overabundance of material from which you may choose as you see fit.

Following are brief descriptions of the contents of these five chapters.

Literary Criticism: Ten Ways to See a Book

Most classroom teachers of literature are familiar and experienced with canonical approaches to literary criticism, the most academically common analytical lenses through which to read and interpret works of creative literature. Most high school students, however, are not. This chapter, the contents of which I have used in my own classroom both as a wholesale preface to a reading of *The Scarlet Letter*, a multiday anticipatory set training students to see the novel from different perspectives, and as a piecemeal, step-by-step lesson scaffolded alongside a reading of the novel, introduces student readers to those common academic approaches to interpretation.

The 10 critical perspectives considered here—the Platonic, Aristotelian, Moralist, Historical-Biographical, Formalist, Rhetorical, Freudian Deconstructionist, Feminist, and Multiculturalist interpretive methodologies—are presented in terms of brief overviews, their respective historical contexts, and their major tenets. Each theory is then paired with a shorter work of American literature that is in some way related to *The Scarlet Letter* and/or its place in the literary canon, offering students the opportunity to "test drive" each interpretive calculus on an isolated piece before utilizing it in approaching Hawthorne's novel. Taken wholly, the contents of this chapter present students with a proverbial "bag of tricks" with which to apprehend more fully the meaning, style, historical importance, and literary value of *The Scarlet Letter* as a masterpiece of American literature.

Reading *The Scarlet Letter*

This chapter is organized chronologically according to the novel's events, containing assignments and assessments tied to particular moments and sections of the plot. It is organized thusly because its focus is on students' initial encounter with and journey through the novel, from the front cover to the back, and its exercises can thus be apportioned out as your class proceeds through the chapters.

The contents of the chapter are divided into four main pedagogical types: ideas for teaching higher level vocabulary through *The Scarlet Letter*; independent journaling questions for each of the novel's chapters, all of which are appropriately assignable as homework and therefore provide a way to differentiate students' interpretation of the plot and Hawthorne's compositional style; brief multiple-choice quizzes formatted to mirror selections from an AP English Literature and Composition exam; and several quotation-based reading and interpretation quizzes, intended both to assess students' recall of the novel's events and to engender discussion of their import. Finally, a lesson plan at the end of the chapter asks students to compare and contrast Hawthorne's own time period with the historical time and place of which he was writing, Puritan Massachusetts.

Understanding *The Scarlet Letter*

This second central chapter contains two distinct approaches to appreciating *The Scarlet Letter* beyond a simple read-through of its plot. The first half of the chapter focuses upon common difficulties that students face when reading Hawthorne's language, particularly its complex and intricate syntactical and otherwise grammatical patterns. In identifying and analyzing many grammatical structures that young readers encounter in the novel, addressing head-on their obvious complexity and related difficulty, I hope to demonstrate ways that you can help students overcome Hawthorne's "language barrier" in order to understand more fully *The Scarlet Letter*'s artistry.

In the chapter's second portion, moreover, I propose several mechanisms by which you can help your students to personalize their understandings of the novel's drama, conflict, themes, and characters. To that end, writing prompts meant to engender bibliotherapy are followed by various worksheets asking students to perform selected tasks and respond to distinctly focused questions, all organized hierarchically according to a generalized taxonomy of cognitive processes. Finally, a lesson plan at the end of the chapter requires students to research and present to one another numerous historical persons, circumstances, and events alluded to throughout *The Scarlet Letter*, augmenting their understanding of the novel on several levels.

Talking About *The Scarlet Letter*

This chapter includes two separate methodologies for engaging students in dialogue concerning the novel: cooperative Socratic seminar discussions and competitive interstudent debates. For each of these two types of dialogic activities, I include detailed explanations of their respective procedures, separate mechanisms (e.g., rubrics and checklists) for evaluating students' participation and success, and numerous topics for discussion from which you can choose. A lesson plan at the end of the chapter asks students to consider and interpret versions and reimaginings of *The Scarlet Letter* on film, on stage, and as separate works of literature, spurring conversation about the novel's thematic importance and potential timelessness.

Writing About *The Scarlet Letter*

As I noted in both of my other *Advanced Placement Classroom* texts, not all essay questions are equivalently aimed, formatted, or administered; this simple fact influenced the organization of this final chapter into six different genres or types of writing assignments. Analytical writing differs from argumentative writing in key ways, and the presentation of research requires distinct compositional approaches from those necessary for creative works of art. Thus, in this chapter, College Board-influenced compositional structure, namely the A-E-C paragraph, is introduced and assessed by way of interpretive worksheets, and 25-minute-long argumentative essays resembling the writing section of the SAT are presented separately from 40-minute-long analytical essays mirroring the essay section of the AP English Literature and Composition exam; all three of these writing assignments are intended for timed, in-class administration. As for take-home assignments, more ponderous, college-length analyses of complex issues related to the novel are dealt with independently of research projects resulting in students' presentations of their findings, and original creative-interpretive projects inviting personalized reflection upon the play constitute a sixth category of assignments. For each of these latter three types of assignments, I include several prompts and/or questions, plus evaluative rubrics and related ideas to improve students' engagement in and learning as a result of the writing process.

Notes on Citations

All excerpts from *The Scarlet Letter* that I quote in my text are taken from the paperback Norton Critical Edition of *The Scarlet Letter and Other Writings* (ISBN 0-393-97953-9), edited by Leland S. Person. All page numbers cited for in-text quotations correspond to the Norton Critical Edition's numeration, with the exception of those excerpts contained on reproducible pages of this book, the line numbers of which are calculated independently.

Additionally, although my parenthetical citations generally follow the APA's guidelines for such, I have retained the literary tradition of citing lines of poetry not according to the pages of text on which they appear, but by the numbers of the quoted lines themselves, as in reproducible materials found within Chapter 2 of this book. Therefore, although a poem's entry in my list of references lists the pages on which that poem appears in its text (e.g., pp. 10–11), I instead cite parenthetically within this book only the lines quoted (e.g., lns. 1–2). As such, any parenthetical citation following a quotation from a poem refers solely to the individual lines that I quote.

Chapter 2

Literary Criticism: Ten Ways to See a Book

What is art, and what is not? Why is one sculpture in a museum, but another relegated to someone's garden? Why is *Romeo and Juliet* still among the most commonly taught books in high schools nationwide, yet *Jurassic Park* is seldom encountered in any scholastic curriculum? Just what is it that separated the Beatles from millions of bands of youngsters in garages across America? My own experience indicates that questions of aesthetic or otherwise artistic quality can be potentially problematic in high school literature courses. On the one hand, answers to such questions are to a degree rather obvious; on the other hand, their answers are often exceedingly difficult to put into words. Sometimes students really do not see why a Shakespearean sonnet is considered more artistically effective than greeting card verse; truth be told, many high schoolers on Valentine's Day would rather be given the latter. Does it not go without saying that the number of teenagers who choose to watch *Hamlet* with their friends on a Friday night is dwarfed by the number who choose the latest slasher horror film or romantic comedy? Doesn't popularity equate to value?

The purpose of this chapter is to provide you with a variety of resources with which to engage in such conversations with your own students, to help them to understand why not all stories are created equally, and moreover that there really is a legitimate reason (or 10) why certain books are truly canonical, whereas others fall short. Most professional educators of the English language arts have engaged in or to some degree utilized literary criticism, either in our own schooling or otherwise. In fact, anyone who has ever read or written an academic essay that analyzes a work of literature is familiar with criticism, for that's really what it is: As I explain it to my own students, literary criticism is just writing about other people's writing.

To a modern teenager, that statement might not seem like a fun, or even very interesting, prospect. Why read what one person wrote about what a different person wrote when you can just go and read the original? Such a response is pragmatically logical, but misses the mark. The value of literary criticism has nothing to do with whether it is written, spoken, or otherwise communicated; on the contrary, the true value of literary criticism is its usefulness.

What Is Meant by the Phrase, "Literary Criticism"

Contrary to common interpretation, the phrase literary criticism does not by its nature have anything to do with disapproval or advice. Just as a food critic is a person who appreciates, understands, and can identify and explain wonderfully prepared cuisine, a literary critic is a person trained with insights into the finer aspects of literature. The word "criticism" is in this sense a synonym for "appreciation" or "analysis."

The student who submits to his or her English teacher a 5-page paper analyzing the symbolic usage of colors in *The Great Gatsby* is therefore to some degree a literary critic. On the other hand, the third grader whose book report recapitulates the plot of *Where the Red Fern Grows* probably does not qualify. Why not, students may ask? Well, is a customer who consistently enjoys one particular establishment's hamburgers a food critic? What if that patron were to submit to the local newspaper an Op-Ed piece describing why he or she loves that restaurant's hamburgers the most? There is a line of definition or qualification, of course, but its location is hard to identify.

As I tell my own students, the issue of who exactly qualifies as a literary critic is for our purposes irrelevant. Pursuing that topic in class may be engaging and interesting, but it is somewhat akin to going on an intellectual snipe hunt. To paraphrase one of my mentors in gifted education, Dr. Joyce VanTassel-Baska, it's not *who* you are, but what you do that counts. Literary criticism is valuable because it is useful to us as readers and interpreters of literature. Analogically, a good critical theory is a tool. If given a simple block of wood, you could saw it, hammer it, drill it, split it, or do any other number of things to it provided that you have the proper tools at your disposal in the first place. Critical theories are to be applied in these ways to works of art.

The 10 Theories of Choice

In addition to the workbench analogy, I have chosen to describe more accurately interpretive critical theories that I have taught to my own classes as lenses through which to examine a work, for whereas tools are destructive or creative (but certainly alter the original materials regardless), a lens is simply an instrument through which to view something. A lens is elucidating, which is what a good critical theory also is. If I look at a painting through clear glass, then I see one thing, but if I look at the same painting through colored or otherwise tinted spectacles, then I see another. Looking at it through a kaleidoscope or 3-D glasses further impacts my view.

Through much of my own literary education, I was introduced to stories firstly for their entertainment value, but additionally for their transmittal of a moral. The story of the three little pigs, for example, is not only a fun yarn, but also warns young readers or listeners about the pitfalls of laziness and overhasty work. As I moved through the grades, works with various historical values were introduced; probably because of my seventh-grade teacher's chosen focus, I recall the setting and historical accuracy of *Johnny Tremain*, but not any particular moral lesson that it contains. *Animal Farm*, in the ninth grade, added metaphoric interpretability to the historical import and moralizing, but *A Tale of Two Cities* in my sophomore year removed symbolism, substituting for it artistically beautiful, admittedly difficult language. I believe that most high school students go through their English language arts educations according to similar interpretive paradigms. Every work of literature taught in school probably has a singular moral, they may believe, in addition to one or two other potentially valuable insights into human history or linguistic creativity.

The Scarlet Letter is, in my opinion, the perfect work with which to break students out of that limiting train of thought. The most canonically revered literature does not have one moral, but many, not a singular point of educative importance, but innumerable ones. The 10 theories outlined by this chapter are of course not the only interpretive methodologies used by or useful to academic readers, but they are all applicable to this particular novel, as well as to most canonical works of literature, at least in my experience. I previously discussed eight of these critical theories in the second edition of *Change Through Choices: A Language Arts Unit for High-Ability Learners* (2010). These earlier expositions of the eight theories appeared on pages 24, 25, 49, 50, 81, 82, 96, and 130 of that unit's Student Guide.

Platonic Literary Theory

In my own AP courses, I always begin with Plato, whose classic *The Republic* aimed for the establishment of a political and social utopia at the expense of art. Students who approach *The Scarlet Letter* according to this theory are able in fact to *criticize* the work according to that word's common understanding. Yes, *The Scarlet Letter* is bad; we should not read it in schools. The reason why, though, has little to do with its "boringness" or "incomprehensibility," but rather with its—and all of art's—potential effects on the peoples and generations of the world.

Aristotelian Literary Theory

Aristotle was Plato's student, and contrary to their intellectual kinship in many veins, they differed in their assessments of the creative arts. *The Scarlet Letter*, Aristotle would have told his teacher, is in fact an extremely valuable piece of literature that should be taught to as many students as possible. Prove it, Plato might have said. The Aristotelian theory attempts to do just that, considering the universal humanity of the novel alongside its potential for bibliotherapy and other forms of emotional catharsis.

Moralist Literary Theory

Placing the growth of literary education in its historical context in the Western world, the materials outlining moralism explain just where we seem to get that old notion that the goal of a scholastic reader should be to find each book's moral lesson. Our culture's traditional emphasis on this task makes historical sense. It is neither right nor wrong, but sensible that our society's initial encounters with literature were moralistic in nature, and *The Scarlet Letter*, set in a forebear of that very society that produced this theory itself, provides much fodder for an application of this interpretive methodology.

Historical-Biographical Literary Theory

Alongside moralism, this critical theory is probably the most commonly applied to *The Scarlet Letter*, for it focuses on the settings of both the story itself and the author who wrote it. The dichotomy of Hawthorne's culture and his tale's separate culture provides much rich material upon which to utilize this particular approach to literary interpretation.

Formalist Literary Theory

Separating the novel itself from the man and context that produced it, formalist theorists would be concerned first and foremost with the story's language: its diction, syntax, punctuation usage, figurative elements, and pace. The architecture of the tale, subdivided into 24 chapters plus a seemingly tangential introduction, is another point of formalist interest, as are the arcs of the plot and conflicts. How the masterpiece is constructed, therefore, becomes of predominant interest to a viewer of *The Scarlet Letter* through this particular lens.

Rhetorical Literary Theory

On the other hand, perhaps the most important and interesting piece of this whole book is in fact the seemingly unrelated "The Custom-House: Introductory to *The Scarlet Letter*" chapter. Why? A rhetorical theorist, concerned with the influences of the author upon the work of literature, requires for his or her investigation a number of details about the author's life, in addition to the creative work itself. Such a rhetorical critic might be interested in Hawthorne's views of his ancestors and how those opinions or insecurities shaped his telling of Hester Prynne's tale. Why did Hawthorne fabricate his story concerning the discovery of the letter and tale? Is there a connection between his employment at Salem's Custom House and his evident dislike of government and church officials, as exhibited in the Puritanical novel? To understand the story, we must firstly understand its author, a rhetorical critic would argue.

Freudian Literary Theory

Viewable perhaps as a grand extension of the rhetorical theory, Freudian literary interpretation relies upon a basic understanding of Sigmund Freud's triadic construct of consciousness (id, ego, and superego), as well as upon his distinction between the conscious and subconscious minds. Dimmesdale, Chillingworth, Hester, and Pearl are all greatly illuminated by an application of this psychoanalytic theory to *The Scarlet Letter*, as potentially the author and his motivation are in addition. Perhaps, Freud might postulate, Hawthorne wrote this entire thing as an act of revenge, an outpouring of shameful contrition, or a stubborn refusal to accede to his ancestors. A very interesting critical lens indeed.

Deconstructionist Literary Theory

Always among my AP students' favorite theories, deconstructionism effectively implodes the book as a whole, at least figuratively. With a gauntlet thrown down to every teacher who has ever told them "your interpretation is wrong," these students delight in their own active roles in the creation of the novel and its meaning, as well as in their own self-reflective insights. What is important about *The Scarlet Letter*? It is only important that I am reading and thinking about it.

Feminist Literary Theory

This particular interpretive approach is quite applicable to *The Scarlet Letter*, which has for generations been interpreted as a work of feminism. The most laudable character is of course Hester, who arises phoenix-like from the ashes of her sin and effectively transforms herself by the denouement into among the most admirable of literary heroines. The male characters are weak, hypocritical, and severely flawed, all dependent upon Hester to play the central role in their salvation or retribution. What, though, are we to make of spritely Pearl and witchy Mistress Hibbins, the only other major female characters in the novel, or of the spitefully cruel but nameless women who twice assemble at Boston's scaffold? Regardless, the novel is full of material to interpret apropos of this theory's approach to literature.

Multicultural Literary Theory

At first glance, this interpretive methodology may seem irrelevant to the novel. After all, there are hardly any minority characters in it. Only some isolated Native Americans, who are themselves described within as savages who live in the forest, which is the place where "the Black Man," a surrogate Satan or devilish character, supposedly resides (p. 79). There are no slaves in the world of *The Scarlet Letter*, although clearly they existed in Puritan Massachusetts. Perhaps the near-total absence of minority characters says more about Hawthorne as author and storytelling architect than it does about the setting itself. Maybe the multicultural literary theory is in fact quite relevant to the novel after all.

How to Use the Contents of This Chapter

Included on pages 20–36 are various reproducible pages outlining, explaining, and applying these 10 critical theories of literary interpretation. These theories are all followed by reproducible worksheets asking students to consider another work of American literature that is in some way relevant to *The Scarlet Letter* or to the study of American literary history, approaching that shorter work via its respective interpretive calculus.

In your own classroom, you may approach the instruction of these 10 theories in several ways. On one hand, you may wish to outline them all for your students preliminarily, prior to reading the novel itself; in this way, your class will have at its disposal a variety of lenses through which to view the proceedings of the book from beginning to end. On the other hand, you may wish to apportion the theories out over your literary unit, perhaps discussing and utilizing the Platonic and

Aristotelian theory after reading Chapter IV, the moralist and historical-biographical theory after reading Chapter VIII, and so on. I have in my own courses over the years instructed via both approaches, and while I generally take the first tack these days, I cannot with certainty say that one instructional approach is better than the other.

Once your students have encountered and utilized these 10 theories, you and they will find them useful in interpreting different literary works, as well. Most canonical literature is analyzable in these ways and in others, so what you are really doing is supplying your class with an interpretive calculus by which to analyze effectively any rich work of literature with which they are presented, on the AP English Literature exam or otherwise. To demonstrate this fact, I have also included on page 37 a brief matching activity requiring students' understanding and application of all 10 literary theories to a single work of unrelated literature, which they may or may not have read previously, William Golding's *Lord of the Flies* (1954/2006). In fact, it may prove better for your instructional purposes if the students have not read this novel, for their successful completion of the matching activity in this case would indicate a clear understanding of the 10 literary theories' interpretive approaches, even when decontextualized from any familiar work of literature.

In the end, students who master these 10 theories of literary interpretation will find their readings of creative literature and their encounters with various works of creative art, most imminently *The Scarlet Letter* itself, to be inherently richer and more substantive.

Chapter Materials

Name: _____   Date: _____

Platonic and Aristotelian Literary Theories

In Ancient Greece, **Plato** believed...	In Ancient Greece, his student **Aristotle** believed...
that literature and other forms of creative art are by their very nature distinct from and inferior to human realities.	that not all art is equally commendable, and there is a distinction to be made between successfully effective literature and the rest.
that such creative products appeal to human emotions, which are sensations and stimuli inferior to and thus less desirable than wisdom, calmness, and reason, which Plato supported.	that the best literature and other works of art in fact succeed impactfully because they imitate the laws and conditions of universal reality, and thus are extremely realistic inherently, thematically, and otherwise.
that dramatists, poets, and other artists should be prohibited from any society which aims for peaceful idealism (e.g., his own Republic, wherein good citizens are nurtured).	that effective poets, dramatists, and other creative artists are in no way dominated by emotion, but are on the contrary simply more in touch with universal truth than are most men.
that literature and other art, because they inflame the passions of their audience, actually undermine reason and calm thought, thereby resulting in societal conflict and ultimately preventing the growth of a utopian Republic.	that "good" literature and art—the lasting kind worth considering—therefore do not harm their audiences by arousing harmful emotions, but instead purge them by effecting benign therapy, illuminating the universals and initiating audiences' emotional catharsis.
that, as a result, poets and artists are unsafe.	that poets and artists are thus useful.

Why Is Any of the Above Information Important to Us?

- Plato and Aristotle were essentially the earliest literary analysts in Western civilization.
- Modern literary criticism is to some degree a direct descendant of these two philosophers' opposing views.
- Their divergent theories represent the two most basic evaluations of literature and art's merits; dichotomously, it's either good or it's bad.
- Aristotle was a student of Plato's, but his assessment of artistic merit, distinct from his forebear's, demonstrates the basic and somewhat paradoxical essence of critical literary theory: any new approach to literary analysis may be at once influenced by past ideas and centrally different than them.

Apply the Theories

Please read the following poem by Anne Bradstreet, the first ever American poet of distinction, who was only the more remarkable because she was a woman writing in Puritan Massachusetts during the 17th century.

"To My Dear and Loving Husband"
Anne Bradstreet (1678)

If ever two were one, then surely we.
If ever man were loved by wife, then thee;
If ever wife was happy in a man,
Compare with me ye women if you can.
I prize thy love more than whole mines of gold,   5
Or all the riches that the East doth hold.
My love is such that rivers cannot quench,
Nor ought but love from thee give recompense.
Thy love is such I can no way repay;
The heavens reward thee manifold, I pray.   10
Then while we live, in love let's so persever,
That when we live no more we may live ever.

How might a Platonic literary critic respond to or interpret this poem?

_____
_____
_____
_____
_____
_____
_____
_____
_____
_____

How might an Aristotelian literary critic respond to or interpret this poem?

_____
_____
_____
_____
_____
_____
_____
_____
_____
_____

Moralist Literary Theory

The first colleges in the United States of America were founded before 1776's Declaration of Independence from Great Britain!

The boys and young men (and at this point of history, only males were allowed) who enrolled in these new colleges and universities in America were educated according to European academic tradition, which was by and large hundreds of years old.

These students in most cases studied philosophy, theology, and divinity. There were no English classes, as we know them today, in American colleges of the early 18th century, so literature would be encountered solely in courses such as these three.

Therefore, until the mid-1800s, there was no such thing in United States academia as an "English professor"; rather, doctors of divinity and theologians were the only conduits for students' encounters with literature at Harvard, Yale, the College of William and Mary, and similar institutions.

Such professors largely thought that creative works of literature should be considered wholly as media for moral education. Thus, these institutional academics believed that if a poem or story was not ethically or outright religiously didactic, then it was not worth including in scholastic curricula.

They by and large disagreed with the idea that creative literature was potentially valuable for communicating an aesthetic or otherwise meaningful experience that could be taken seriously for its own sake.

In your opinion, does this approach to literature more closely resemble the Platonic or Aristotelian theory? Why?

Name: _____ Date: _____

Historical-Biographical Literary Theory

By the mid-1800s, in many American and European colleges, English as an academic field was attempting to distinguish itself from more strictly moralistic disciplines such as divinity, philosophy, and theology. Various professors began, in fact, to request of their institutions of higher education opportunities to establish independent departments of English.

Most traditional institutional administrations immediately refused such proposals, recoiling especially from the idea that literature was somehow valuable in and of itself, rather than as a means to a spiritual end, but before long, would-be English professors were allowed to propose their ideas and departmental constructs further.

Ultimately, the only way that many institutional powers would allow English departments their independence was if the professors labored to make literary study "scientific."

From this requirement arose the Historical-Biographical literary model, otherwise known as Historicism. This approach to literature essentially necessitated a complex search for historical facts and facets of literary works, and the early English departments that propagated it trained readers of literature as if they were forensic scientists.

Historical-Biographical critics see works of creative literature chiefly as reflections of their authors' and poets' lives and times or of the works' own historical settings.

According to Historicism, a thoroughly enriched reading of a work of literature depends upon knowing and reflecting upon the timbres of the times when the work was either written or set, including:

- its intellectual movements,
- its artistic currents,
- its politics,
- its economic conditions,
- its social trends, and
- the author's private affairs.

There is certainly merit to this way of thinking about literature, but there are also some shortcomings:
- this approach to creative literature effectively turns art into history—a document of the past—rather than something that is still alive and important in the present; and
- it disengages English students from the works of literature that they study; to wit, students might become too busy searching for the political or social influences behind a given poem to read considerately and thoroughly the poem itself! This obviously reduces literature's inherent meaning and value.

Nevertheless, in institutions of higher education throughout the English-speaking world, the academic paradigms of Moralism and Historicism dominated the discipline of literary scholarship until the radical upheaval of the Roaring '20s.

Apply the Theories

Please read the following poem by Phillis Wheatley, a Massachusetts slave who was brought to the United States at the age of 7; by the age of 20, she had been taught and mastered the English language to such a degree that she was a published and esteemed poet.

Literary Criticism: Ten Ways to See a Book

Name: _____ Date: _____

"On Being Brought From Africa to America"
Phillis Wheatley (1768, 1773)

'Twas mercy brought me from my pagan land,
Taught my benighted soul to understand
That there's a God, that there's a Savior too:
Once I redemption neither sought nor knew.
Some view our sable race with scornful eye,
"Their color is a diabolic dye."
Remember Christians; Negroes, black as Cain,
May be refin'd, and join th' angelic train.

How might a moralist literary critic respond to this poem?

_____
_____
_____
_____
_____
_____
_____
_____
_____
_____
_____
_____

How might a historical-biographical literary critic respond to this poem?

_____
_____
_____
_____
_____
_____
_____
_____
_____
_____
_____
_____

Formalist Literary Theory

In 16th-, 17th-, and 18th-century colleges and universities, Moralism was the most common approach to literary interpretation

In the mid-19th century, the Historical-Biographical theory arose and spread

By the 1920s, however, an emergent critical philosophy arose within academic establishments: the Formalist Literary Theory.

Formalism is in many ways an oppositional response to the scientifically critical approach proposed by Historicism.

The central tenet of Formalism, in direct contrast to Historicism, is that any effective or otherwise "good" work of literature and other creative art is an organic whole, free from any necessary underpinnings of its author and his or her society. In other words, once a literary work is put down on paper, then *that's* where it exists . . . not the author's mind, society, or time period.

According to this Formalist theory of literary interpretation, then, a good reader, in order to understand a work of literature fully, must consider the following aspects of it:

- its architectural structure and unity,
- the interrelationships of its component parts,
- its diction and syntax, and
- its artistic style and resultant contribution to the meaning.

For these reasons, Formalism can be encapsulated in brief by these two succinct statements:
- **How** a work of literature means is as important as **what** it means.
- Meritorious works of literature are valuable chiefly for their human and otherwise literary content, not for who wrote them, where, or when.

Name: _____ Date: _____

Rhetorical Literary Theory

Just as Plato's negative consideration of literature and creative art prompted a rebuttal and alternate theory from Aristotle in ancient Greece, so in 1920s academia did the proposals of Formalist literary critics do likewise, prompting the arisal of the Rhetorical Literary Theory.

The theory's label comes from the root morpheme "*rhetor*," meaning "speaker" or "orator," for:

- Rhetorical theorists believe it naïve to try to view or consider any work of art as some sort of autonomous creation because it was, and remains, the conscious creation of a human being possessing his or her own thought processes.
- Even writers and other creators who aim for artistic objectivity can never excise themselves and their perspectives completely.
- Therefore, the beliefs, background, and personality of an author should *never* be ignored because they will always be pertinent to the meanings of his or her creative products.
- When any reader encounters a work of literature, as a result, its author is always there, attempting to persuade his or her readership according to his or her own personal value systems and ideologies.
- Yes, it *is* important to read a work of literature very closely, but always considering how the diction, syntax, form, style, and unity of the work communicate somehow its author's own personal beliefs, even if unintentionally so.

Consider, for example, the following hypothetical authorial situation:

If Phillis Wheatley were to write a poem as if she were Anne Bradstreet, writing throughout the poem, in every way possible, as if she actually were Bradstreet, then the ultimate creator of the poem would be…

still Phillis Wheatley.

Even if written from the perspective of another woman, that particular poem would still represent the life experiences, perspectives, artistic choices, and influential ideologies of Phillis Wheatley.

This literary theory resembles Historicism in its consideration of extraneous influence upon creative works, but the Rhetorical theory is concerned solely with the author's influence, intentional or otherwise, rather than society's.

Apply the Theory

Please read the opening to the United States' 1776 Declaration of Independence from Great Britain, as follows.

> When, in the course of human events, it becomes necessary for one people to dissolve the political bands which have connected them with another, and to assume among the powers of the earth, the separate and equal station to which the laws of nature and of nature's God entitle them, a decent respect to the opinions of mankind requires that they should declare the causes which impel them to the separation.
> We hold these truths to be self-evident, that all men are created equal, that they are endowed by their Creator with certain unalienable rights, that among these are life, liberty and the pursuit of happiness. That to secure these rights, governments are instituted among men, deriving their just powers from the consent of the governed. That whenever any form of government becomes destructive to these ends, it is the right of the people to alter or to abolish it, and to institute new

government, laying its foundation on such principles and organizing its powers in such form, as to them shall seem most likely to effect their safety and happiness. Prudence, indeed, will dictate that governments long established should not be changed for light and transient causes; and accordingly all experience hath shown that mankind are more disposed to suffer, while evils are sufferable, than to right themselves by abolishing the forms to which they are accustomed. But when a long train of abuses and usurpations, pursuing invariably the same object evinces a design to reduce them under absolute despotism, it is their right, it is their duty, to throw off such government, and to provide new guards for their future security.

How might a Formalist literary critic interpret this excerpt's form and style?

How might a Rhetorical literary critic respond to this excerpt, acknowledging its writing by Thomas Jefferson, Virginian slave-owner?

Freudian Literary Theory

The father of psychoanalytic literary criticism, Sigmund Freud was actually not a professor of literature at all, but rather an independent medical psychologist in Austria.

His years of independent practice in the late 19th and early 20th centuries led him to postulate a unique psychical structure of human consciousness. Specifically, Freud theorized that humans actually had two levels of mental consciousness:

- The Conscious Level
    - perceivable by human thinkers ... we are aware of it
    - the level on which we think about and feel things

- The Subconscious Level
    - not perceivable by human thinkers ... we are unaware of its contents and workings
    - blank and without form at birth, like a white canvas without paint on it yet
    - imprinted throughout life by a person's thoughts, emotions, and experiences
    - its contents and patterns are accessible only through hypnosis and dream analysis

Freud also believed that, within that conscious/subconscious psychological dichotomy, human thought is composed of three critical parts:

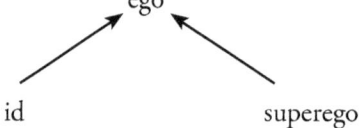

- One's *id* is the pleasure-seeker, the source of the libido's flow into the psyche, energetically concerned solely with the search for happiness and fulfillment

- One's *superego* is the agent of the demands, concerns, and pressures of society and of role models, and as such is the source of a person's morality and/or guilt

- One's *ego* receives impulses and directions from both the *id* and the *superego*; it is the center of a mind's rational awareness—its decision-maker—and thus makes choices and directs actions based on the urges of the *id* and *superego*.

All three parts of this psychical triad exist partially on the conscious level and partially on the subconscious level of human thought; among the three, one's *ego* exists most prominently on the conscious level, as its decision maker.

To illustrate, consider the case of a student who must complete a project for school, but would rather go to the beach. Although this student knows that his or her parents, teachers, and friends will all be disappointed if he or she does not earn a good grade, what he or she really wants to do is relax in the sun and splash in the waves.

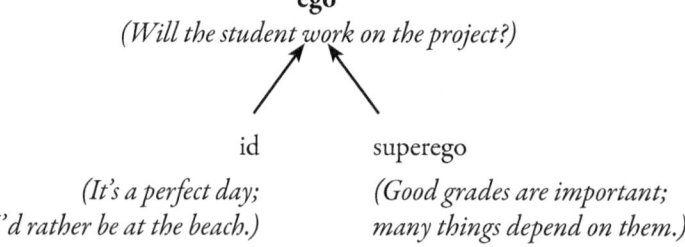

The Scarlet Letter

Name: _____ Date: _____

This situation exemplifies a relatively simple conflict for the *ego* to resolve, but sometimes the impulses of a person's *id* are too blatantly in conflict with the *superego*. In such cases, one's *ego* and *superego* work together to force the "unacceptable" desires from the *id* down into a person's subconscious so that they no longer make conscious demands of the *ego*. Such psychical defense mechanisms (called *censors*) can take these forms, among others:

- repression of impulses,
- rationalization of impulses, and
- projection/displacement of impulses onto seemingly unrelated people or objects.

After the repressive work of the *censor*, one's "unacceptable" desires are no longer perceivable on the conscious level, yet just as powerful and influential to the *ego*, albeit "undercover" subconsciously.

Additionally, Freudian theorists believe that the *id* deals with two opposing instincts:

- *Eros*, the life instinct, which is concerned with pleasure and the creation of life
- *Thanatos*, the death instinct, commonly called one's "death wish," which desires self-mutilation and self-destruction

But what does any of this psychoanalytic theory and terminology have to do with literature?

An understanding of Freud' theorized psychological structure is relevant to literary criticism in several ways:

- Freudian psychologists believe that creativity in general is a form of *censoring* "unacceptable" impulses from the *id*, channeling desires incompatible with the expectations and pressures of society into accepted, productive, and ultimately cathartic artistic areas. Thus, this theory proposes that artists by and large create art in order to satisfy the conflicting demands of their *ids* and *superegos*.

- All sorts of neuroses, meaning any intellectual conditions that are abnormal relative to the beliefs and practices of one's society, are perhaps formed when a person is for some reason unable to move "unacceptable" desires from the *id* into his or her subconscious, a mental blockage of some sort impeding the work of the *censor*. Thus, per this theory, serial killers act as they do because their *egos* and *superegos* are prevented from enacting *censors* to "get rid of" their unacceptable desires; in other words, this theory postulates that they are mentally prevented from *not* killing. Keep in mind, though, that these ideas are strictly theoretical.

Apply the Theory

Please read the following poem by Anne Bradstreet, the first ever American poet of distinction, who was only the more remarkable because she was a woman writing in Puritan Massachusetts during the 17th century.

"The Author to Her Book"
Anne Bradstreet (1678)

Thou ill-formed offspring of my feeble brain,
Who after birth did'st by my side remain,
Till snatcht from thence by friends, less wise than true,
Who thee abroad exposed to public view,
Made thee in rags, halting to th' press to trudge,   5

Name: _____   Date: _____

Where errors were not lessened (all may judge).
At thy return my blushing was not small,
My rambling brat (in print) should mother call.
I cast thee by as one unfit for light,
The visage was so irksome in my sight,   *10*
Yet being mine own, at length affection would
Thy blemishes amend, if so I could.
I washed thy face, but more defects I saw,
And rubbing off a spot, still made a flaw.
I stretcht thy joints to make thee even feet,   *15*
Yet still thou run'st more hobbling than is meet.
In better dress to trim thee was my mind,
But nought save home-spun cloth, i' th' house I find.
In this array, 'mongst vulgars may'st thou roam.
In critic's hands, beware thou dost not come,   *20*
And take thy way where yet thou art not known.
If for thy father askt, say, thou hadst none;
And for thy mother, she alas is poor,
Which caused her thus to send thee out of door.

How might a Freudian literary theorist respond to or interpret this poem?

_____
_____
_____
_____
_____
_____
_____
_____
_____
_____
_____
_____
_____
_____
_____
_____
_____
_____
_____
_____

Name: _____ Date: _____

Deconstructionist Literary Theory

Deconstructionism is perhaps the most philosophical literary theory existent today. It arose in the early 20th century from French philosophers who questioned the existence of absolute reality, idealizing "reality" as we know it as a social and/or personal construct.

This theory hinges on the understanding that language—all language—is metaphoric, having no absolute and necessary connection with anything beyond itself. In other words,

- There is no fixed link between the color yellow and the word "yellow."
- There is no necessary reason why that specific color could not as easily be called "red," or "cherry," or "Timbuktu," or "chyanghendholph," or whatever.
- We as human beings associate the color with the word "yellow" only because other human beings, our peers and historical forefathers, agreed that we should.

The natural correlate follows that all language, specifically diction, is therefore arbitrary. Each reader of a given word carries with himself or herself a personal set of subjective metaphors, impressions, images, and interpretations. For example:

If everyone in a classroom were to close his or her eyes and listen while the teacher were to say the word "fire," then the images and connotations with which each student would mentally respond would be totally unique, distinct from all other students' responses.

- Some would picture a blazing building, some a campfire, and others a small burner.
- Some would feel fear, some would feel happiness, and others would feel intrigued.
- The meaning of the particular word "fire" is thus arbitrary.
- It means all of the above, and none of the above.

Therefore, Deconstructionist analysts believe that there is no true "right" or "wrong" interpretive reading of a work of literature or anything else, as one person's independent set of linguistic metaphoric associations is just as valid as any other person's.

The most important result of literary criticism, evaluation, and analysis, a Deconstructionist thus concludes, is an understanding of and appreciation for how a given work of literature *makes you as a reader think and feel*, how you as an individual respond to the work. Every other interpretation is truly irrelevant and incomprehensible.

In fact, some Deconstructionists argue, a work of literature is because of this arbitrariness not a creation solely of its author, for each reader of literature is just as necessary to create meaning from it as the person who originally wrote it down. In other words,

Nathaniel Hawthorne's words really mean nothing if you do not take them off the shelf, read them, and think about them.

Apply the Theory

Please read the following excerpt from Ralph Waldo Emerson's *Nature*. Emerson was a contemporary and friend of Nathaniel Hawthorne's, as well as one of the most important figures of Transcendentalism.

from *Nature*
Ralph Waldo Emerson (1836)

A third use which Nature subserves to man is that of Language. Nature is the vehicle of thought, and in a simple, double, and three-fold degree.

Words are signs of natural facts.

Particular natural facts are symbols of particular spiritual facts.

Nature is the symbol of the spirit.

Words are signs of natural facts. The use of natural history is to give us aid in supernatural history. The use of the outer creation is to give us language for the beings and changes of the inward creation. Every word which is used to express a moral or intellectual fact, if traced to its root, is found to be borrowed from some material appearance. *Right* originally means *straight*; *wrong* means *twisted*. *Spirit* primarily means *wind*; *transgression*, the crossing of a *line*; *supercilious*, the *raising of the eye-brow*. We say the *heart* to express emotion, the *head* to denote thought; and *thought* and *emotion* are, in their turn, words borrowed from sensible things, and now appropriated to spiritual nature. Most of the process by which this transformation is made, is hidden from us in the remote time when language was framed; but the same tendency may be daily observed in children. Children and savages use only nouns or names of things, which they continually convert into verbs, and apply to analogous mental acts.

How would a Deconstructionist critic, namely you, respond to this poem?

Name: _____ Date: _____

Feminist Literary Theory

Feminist literary critics believe that gender is central to life, and thus that attention to gender must be paid when examining both life and literature. To ignore "gender studies" when reading, studying, and analyzing literature is simply a naïve and incomplete approach, they contend.

Over the years (largely the last 50 or so), feminist critics have primarily concerned themselves with three focal studies of literature:

- The representation of female characters in a text, including:
    - their treatment within and by the culture of the text/story (i.e., how does the society of the story treat its females, and why?)
    - their treatment by the text's male characters (i.e., how do the males in a particular story treat female characters, and why?)
    - the relationships among the women in the text (i.e., how do the female characters in a story treat each other, both (a) in strictly female groups and (b) in groups composed of both males and females, and why?)

- The place of female writers in the literary canon
- The ways in which men and women readers respond differently to literature (this aspect of feminist criticism is partly literary and partly sociological or psychological)

It is an undeniable fact that societal divisions by gender affect the legal, economic, and social lives of women in our modern world, as well as women's ways of perceiving and acting in that world, just as they have in centuries past.

Feminist criticism often aims at liberating society from narrow gender-based limitations; thus, it is notable as an academic approach to literary criticism with an end-goal beyond intellectual academia.

Please note the overlaps between feminist literary theory and multiculturalism.

Apply the Theory

Please read the following description of Sarah Pierrepont by Jonathan Edwards, a Puritan minister from Connecticut who is in some ways responsible for the genesis of America's "Great Awakening."

"Sarah Pierrepont"
Jonathan Edwards (1723?)

They say there is a young lady in [New Haven] who is beloved of that almighty Being, who made and rules the world, and that there are certain seasons in which this great Being, in some way or other invisible, comes to her and fills her mind with exceeding sweet delight, and that she hardly cares for anything, except to meditate on him—that she expects after a while to be received up where he is, to be raised up out of the world and caught up into heaven; being assured that he loves her too well to let her remain at a distance from him always. There she is to dwell with him, and to be ravished with his love and delight forever. Therefore, if you present all the world before her, with the richest of its treasures, she disregards it and cares not for it, and is unmindful of any pain or affliction. She has a strange sweetness in her mind, and singular purity in her affections; is most just and conscientious in all her actions; and you could not persuade her to do anything wrong or sinful, if you would give her all the world, lest she should offend this great Being. She is of a wonderful sweetness, calmness and universal benevolence of mind; especially after those seasons in which this great God has manifested himself to her mind. She will sometimes go about from place to place, singing sweetly; and seems to be always of joy and pleasure; and no one knows for what. She loves to be alone, and to wander in the fields and on the mountains, and seems to have someone invisible always conversing with her.

- How might a Feminist literary critic respond to this sermonized description?

Name: _____ Date: _____

Multicultural Literary Theory

Multicultural critics believe that race and culture are central to life, and thus attention to heterogeneous cultures must be paid when examining both life and literature. They contend that to ignore cultures other than the dominant one(s)—or to pay attention solely to any singular race or culture—when reading, studying, and analyzing literature is simply a naïve and incomplete approach.

Over the years (largely the last 50 or so), multicultural critics have primarily concerned themselves with three focal studies of literature:

- The representation of racial/cultural minority characters in a text, including:
    - their treatment within and by the world of the text/story (i.e., how does the society of the story treat its—at least in the Western world—non-Whites, and why?)
    - their treatment by the text's characters who are members of the cultural or racial majority (i.e., how do—at least in the Western world—the White characters in a particular story treat non-White characters, and why?)
    - the relationships among multicultural characters in the text (i.e., how do characters who are not members of the cultural majority in a particular text treat each other, both (a) in groups representing strictly their own culture and (b) in groups composed of members of several racial cultures, and why?)

- The place of multicultural (i.e., non-White) writers in the literary canon
- The ways in which readers of different races and cultures respond differently to literature (this aspect of multiculturalism is partly literary and partly sociological or psychological)

It is an undeniable fact that societal divisions by culture and race affect the legal, economic, and social lives of individuals and groups of people in our modern world, as well as multicultural persons' ways of perceiving and acting in that world, just as they have in centuries past.

Multicultural critics often aim (a) to understand more clearly the racial and cultural lines dividing our heterogeneous society, and (b) at liberating society from narrow race-based limitations; like feminism, it is therefore an academically interpretive methodology with an end-goal beyond academia.

- Thinking about both American and Western history, why does it make sense that feminism and multiculturalism have only been part of mainstream academia for the last 50 years or so?

_____
_____
_____
_____
_____
_____
_____
_____
_____
_____

Name: _____ Date: _____

Apply the Theory

Please read the following poem by Lydia Howard Huntley Sigourney, a popular writer of newspaper verse who in this work considers a greeting of Pilgrim colonists by a native American, apocryphally on March 16, 1622.

"The Indian's Welcome to the Pilgrim Fathers"
Lydia Howard Huntley Sigourney (1835)

Above them spread a stranger sky
Around, the sterile plain,
The rock-bound coast rose frowning nigh,
Beyond, - the wrathful main:
Chill remnants of the wintry snow 5
Still chok'd the encumber'd soil,
Yet forth these Pilgrim fathers go,
To mark their future toil.

'Mid yonder vale their corn must rise
In Summer's ripening pride, 10
And there the church-spire woo the skies
Its sister-school beside.
Perchance 'mid England's velvet green
Some tender thought repos'd,—
Though nought upon their stoic mien 15
Such soft regret disclos'd.

When sudden from the forest wide
A red-brow'd chieftain came,
With towering form, and haughty stride,
And eye like kindling flame: 20

No wrath he breath'd, no conflict sought,
To no dark ambush drew,
But simply to the Old World brought,
The welcome of the New.

That welcome was a blast and ban 25
Upon thy race unborn.
Was there no seer, thou fated Man!
Thy lavish zeal to warn?
Thou in thy fearless faith didst hail
A weak, invading, band 30
But who shall heed thy children's wail,
Swept from their native land?

Thou gav'st the riches of thy streams,
The lordship o'er thy waves
The region of thy infant dreams, 35
And of thy father's graves,
But who to yon proud mansions pil'd
With wealth of earth and sea,
Poor outcast from thy forest wild,
Say, who shall welcome thee? 40

How might a Multicultural literary critic respond to this poem?

_____
_____
_____
_____
_____
_____
_____
_____

Name: _____   Date: _____

How the 10 Literary Theories Look in Practice

Please match the types of critics/theorists to their respective interpretations of *Lord of the Flies*.

Potential Answers
- a. a Platonic critic's reaction
- b. an Aristotelian critic's reaction
- c. a Moralist critic's reaction
- d. a Historical-Biographical critic's reaction
- e. a Formalist critic's reaction
- f. a Rhetorical critic's reaction
- g. a Freudian critic's reaction
- h. a Deconstructionist critic's reaction
- i. a Feminist critic's reaction
- j. a Multicultural critic's reaction

1. _____ This critic interprets *Lord of the Flies*, and particularly Simon's massacre by members of his own tribe, as a Biblical allegory, inferring ultimately that the novel is a treatise against polytheism and the sacrifice of valuable goods to imaginary idols, such as the demonic Beast.

2. _____ This critic examines various parallels between the events of *Lord of the Flies* and the political arc of World War II, suggesting (a) that *Lord of the Flies* was written to allegorize the recently ended war, (b) that numerous characters in the novel resemble political players in World War II, (c) that *Lord of the Flies* can thus be interpreted as legitimate political commentary on the war-ravaged time when it was written, and (d) that the novel in this way parallels numerous political cartoons that appeared in the *London Times* during the 1940s.

3. _____ This critic is particularly concerned with the metaphors and similes that appear in *Lord of the Flies*; through an extended examination of symbols, he or she proposes that the novel ultimately leads the reader through a figurative calculus associating Earth and Water with safety and goodness, but Fire and Air with danger, fear, and evil.

4. _____ This critic focuses on *Lord of the Flies*'s chief antagonist, Jack. Specifically, this critic interprets Jack's descent into madness as the engenderment of a true neurosis, for while Jack's superego is strong and prohibitive at the beginning of the novel, by its end his superego and ego are unable to censor the murderous, cruel impulses of his id, which ultimately runs amuck uninhibited; moreover, this critic posits, Jack's increasingly common dialogue with the other boys regarding the imaginary Beast is a creative outlet for the stress caused by conflict between his English-trained superego and his power-hungry id. Ultimately, then, the novel serves as a demonstration of the ways in which *thanatos*, the "death wish" side of one's id, overtakes social and personal restraint in the absence of formal authority.

5. _____ This critic examines the fracturing of the boys into separate tribes in *Lord of the Flies*, particularly how such separation occurs and how the tribes think about and respond to each other following the schism. He or she in this way uses *Lord of the Flies* as a literary mirror on which to examine human cultures' compulsion to fear, neglect, and/or demonize "otherness," and ultimately to attack such racial and cultural "others" with the ultimate aim of subjugation or annihilation. The critic uses elements of both dialogue and plot to interpret *Lord of the Flies* in this way as a portrayal of racial and cultural fragmentation.

6. _____ This critic considers the ways in which all of the boys on the island in *Lord of the Flies* might act differently were there any girls present. He or she hypothesizes that the Littluns would be much better cared for in such a case, while the Biguns would antagonize each other more quickly due to competition for female attention; this hypothesis is supported in this critic's analysis by sociological studies examining interactions between males and females of different ages in isolated, stressful situations.

7. _____ This critic attempts to tie the publication of *Lord of the Flies* in the 1950s to the social unrest that arose in American and British society in following decades; effectively, this critic posits, the publication of *Lord of the Flies* contributed in part to the social revolutions and anti-government sentiments of the late 1960s.

8. _____ This critic examines how William Golding's personal experiences both during adolescence and during World War II led him to write *Lord of the Flies*; he or she proposes that Golding's portrayal of human nature and cruelty in the novel are depictions of behavior that he either engaged in or observed during these two critical times of his own life, as based on textual, descriptive evidence from both the novel and Golding's own diary and correspondences.

9. _____ This critic analyzes one scene in *Lord of the Flies*: Simon's murder by his rampaging peers on the beach. He or she begins by investigating the diction used to describe (a) Simon's murder, (b) the parachutist's descent following the murder, and (c) Simon's departure to the ocean, escorted by translucent creatures. The critic recounts predominant theories interpreting this particular scene as Biblical and/or spiritual in nature, then attempts to debunk them all by demonstrating how language in this scene can be interpreted in various other ways, most amusingly suggesting (a) that Simon might be abducted by an alien visitor at this point, and (b) that the phosphorescent creatures mentioned could actually be read as disembodied souls of the murderous boys, circling around the figurative embodiment of their collective loneliness. Overall, this critic's main goal seems to be an exposition of other analyses' shortcomings.

10. _____ This critic is concerned with Golding's use of the snake as a symbol of evil in *Lord of the Flies*. He or she compares the novel's portrayal of serpent-like creatures to similar depictions in Biblical, Hopi Indian, Germanic, and Middle Eastern folktales, using all of these occurrences to conclude that the boys' fear and discussion of snakes is in line with the tradition of ancient worldly wisdom literature.

Answer Key for Matching Activity

1. This interpretation's emphasis on religion and moral didacticism imply that it accords with the views of theorist C.
2. This interpretation focuses on parallels between the novel and historical events and figures; it is thus an example of the work of theorist D.
3. This interpretation does not concern itself with the author of the novel, the setting of the novel, the historical period that produced the work, etc. Instead, it relies upon an apparently deep and thorough reading of symbols (i.e., solely of things appearing in the text), thereby indicating that it results from theorist E.
4. The psychological approach and language used in this interpretation to investigate the novel are substantial clues that this analysis came from theorist G.
5. This analysis of the novel compares social division in the novel to social and cultural division in reality, ultimately concluding that *Lord of the Flies* mimics racial and cultural separations and struggles in the real world, indicating that it is a product of theorist J.
6. This interpretation's focus on absent female figures and the hypothetical effect that such characters would have on the novel's status quo indicate that it is the work of theorist I.
7. This hypothesis attempts to tie the work of imaginative literature itself to social upheaval that occurred in reality following the work's publication, implying that its origin was theorist A.
8. The usage of an author's personal history, records, and correspondences in order to make sense of a work of literature indicate a belief that artists' personal lives shape their creative works, thereby indicating that this interpretation is from theorist F.
9. This analysis is confusing, yes, but two notable facts—(a) it relies upon the ambiguity of diction and (b) it is playful in demonstrating how literature can be interpreted in multiple, equally legitimate ways—indicate that it is a product of theorist H.
10. The ultimate aim of this interpretation is to demonstrate how *Lord of the Flies*, at least in one particular way, is fully in line with the universal storytelling tradition; as such, it accords with the ideology of theorist B.

Chapter 3

Reading *The Scarlet Letter*

This chapter includes activities, assignments, and various reproducible materials intended to aid students through the initial process of reading *The Scarlet Letter*. Unlike other chapters to come, this one is organized according to the forward movement of the novel's plot, chronologically, as students' reading will proceed from the front of the book to the back. I have designed the included prompts and materials not only to enhance students' understanding of the plot and characters, but also to require engagement of the text and higher level thinking, thereby preparing them for the deeper analysis and insight expected on the AP Literature and Composition Exam. Specifically, I have included in this chapter the following pedagogical components: an approach to and resources for vocabulary analysis, chapter-by-chapter independent journaling questions, AP-style multiple choice quizzes, various reading quizzes requiring close attention and quotation analysis, and a stand-alone lesson plan requiring students to compare and contrast Hawthorne's 19th century America with Puritan Massachusetts.

Vocabulary Analysis

Among the major difficulties faced by student readers fresh to Nathaniel Hawthorne is a trouble with comprehension, often arising from his sometimes admittedly difficult diction. Like Charles Dickens, John Milton, and the great William Shakespeare, Hawthorne interjects an abundance of high-level vocabulary into his works, the difficulty of which is potentially enhanced for modern readers because of some words' archaic qualities. Thus, encountering and fully examining *The Scarlet Letter* in school provides students with an opportunity to improve their own vocabularies by leaps and bounds, as well as their understanding of the choices that authors make in selecting particular words contextually.

I personally believe that linguistic instruction, especially if focused on vocabulary building, is enhanced when it is student-directed, centered upon, and drawn from the taught literary curriculum, so I have on page 50 included a vocabulary analysis worksheet in the Chapter Materials section for this chapter, which students can use as a template for their investigations of diction.

As students read through *The Scarlet Letter*, they should identify and collect words that they find interesting, cryptic, or otherwise important, then utilize this analytical mechanism as a device for further investigation and analysis of their chosen words. Additionally, I have compiled a list of words that readers commonly find confusing; you may wish to assign the investigation of these words to your students and require their interpretation using the vocabulary worksheet prior to reading the chapters in which they arise, thereby preempting your students' potential difficulties in reading comprehension.

Moreover, there are several creative ways in which classroom teachers might publicize or share students' vocabulary analysis work, possibly helping your entire class to benefit from the scholarship of its individual members. Visible bulletin boards, simple pair-and-shares, compiled vocabulary folios or novel-centered-dictionaries, and oral presentations to one's own or other classes are all feasible and useful options for spreading students' vocabulary research across their classes.

A vocabulary list, including reference points to where each word occurs in the text, is provided on the next page.

Journaling Questions

When I teach books of all kinds—plays, novels, etc.—to my own AP English Literature students, I consistently ask them to complete journaling assignments on nights when they read for homework. Reading quizzes on days following nightly homework assignments are useful, but do not by themselves effectively ensure students' full and attentive engagement with each night's assigned section. On the other hand, requiring that students respond analytically to those reading assignments establishes a norm that your pupils not only comprehend the text when read, but also collect and analyze particularly important portions of each assignment, preparing on a nightly basis for the exegeses required by the AP exam itself. The simple act of reading a chapter or two for homework in this way becomes an exercise in interpreting characters' motivations, tones, and actions; paying close attention to symbolism and literary devices; mining the text for important details; and ultimately reporting one's findings in organized, supported mini-essays.

TABLE 3
Vocabulary Study Words for The Scarlet Letter

edifice ("Custom-House")	commiseration (Ch. 5)	retribution (Ch. 14)
decorous ("Custom-House")	efficacy (Ch. 6)	behest (Ch. 14)
languid ("Custom-House")	mutability (Ch. 6)	verdure (Ch. 15)
prolix ("Custom-House")	inscrutable (Ch. 6)	sedulous (Ch. 15)
arduous ("Custom-House")	gesticulation (Ch. 6)	petulant (Ch. 15)
detriment ("Custom-House")	amenable (Ch. 6)	precocity (Ch. 15)
emolument ("Custom-House")	enmity (Ch. 6)	beneficence (Ch. 15)
cumbrous ("Custom-House")	eminence (Ch. 7)	vivacity (Ch. 15)
impunity ("Custom-House")	intrinsic (Ch. 7)	loquacity (Ch. 16)
liberality ("Custom-House")	imperious (Ch. 7)	lamentation (Ch. 16)
torpid ("Custom-House")	cabalistic (Ch. 7)	scintillate (Ch. 16)
discourtesy ("Custom-House")	embowed (Ch. 7)	contiguity (Ch. 17)
truculent ("Custom-House")	exigency (Ch. 7)	misanthropy (Ch. 17)
eulogium ("Custom-House")	relinquish (Ch. 7)	consecration (Ch. 17)
vitiate ("Custom-House")	expatiate (Ch. 8)	estrange (Ch. 18)
polemical ("Custom-House")	unfeignedly (Ch. 8)	colloquy (Ch. 18)
lucubration ("Custom-House")	benevolence (Ch. 8)	subjugate (Ch. 18)
edifice (Ch. 1)	emaciated (Ch. 8)	denizen (Ch. 18)
sepulchre (Ch. 1)	vehemence (Ch. 8)	accost (Ch. 19)
ponderous (Ch. 1)	unobtrusive (Ch. 8)	mollified (Ch. 19)
congenial (Ch. 1)	appellation (Ch. 9)	preternatural (Ch. 19)
inauspicious (Ch. 1)	countenance (Ch. 9)	vicissitude (Ch. 20)
betokened (Ch. 2)	propound (Ch. 9)	irrefragable (Ch. 20)
indubitably (Ch. 2)	erudition (Ch. 9)	obeisance (Ch. 20)
heterodox (Ch. 2)	commodiousness (Ch. 9)	potentate (Ch. 20)
venerable (Ch. 2)	emissary (Ch. 9)	gratuitous (Ch. 20)
transgressor (Ch. 2)	inimical (Ch. 10)	requite (Ch. 20)
infamy (Ch. 2)	abasement (Ch. 10)	comport (Ch. 20)
malefactor (Ch. 2)	decorously (Ch. 10)	effervesce (Ch. 21)
sumptuary (Ch. 2)	palliate (Ch. 10)	probity (Ch. 21)
ignominy (Ch. 2)	somniferous (Ch. 10)	tempestuous (Ch. 21)
remonstrance (Ch. 2)	odious (Ch. 11)	animadversion (Ch. 21)
heterogeneous (Ch. 3)	machination (Ch. 11)	gradation (Ch. 22)
sojourn (Ch. 3)	attestation (Ch. 11)	indefatigable (Ch. 22)
iniquity (Ch. 3)	impalpable (Ch. 11)	unscrupulous (Ch. 22)
sagacity (Ch. 3)	defunct (Ch. 12)	surmise (Ch. 22)
tremulous (Ch. 3)	scurrilous (Ch. 12)	apotheosis (Ch. 23)
fervor (Ch. 3)	malevolence (Ch. 12)	transitory (Ch. 23)
amenable (Ch. 4)	semblance (Ch. 13)	intimation (Ch. 23)
peremptory (Ch. 4)	obviate (Ch. 13)	conjectural (Ch. 24)
vivify (Ch. 5)	ethereal (Ch. 13)	portent (Ch. 24)
uncongenial (Ch. 5)	acquiesce (Ch. 13)	bequeathed (Ch. 24)
progenitor (Ch. 5)	propinquity (Ch. 14)	recluse (Ch. 24)

Reading The Scarlet Letter

I personally do not grade such journal entries using any sort of extraneous rubric, but instead simply and swiftly evaluate students' responses based upon three simple criteria: length and depth, their utilization of textual support, and the "correctness" of their analyses. Entries are awarded numerical scores for "L/D," "TS," and "C," together composing a single homework grade for each nightly assignment. The last evaluative criterion—correctness—is, of course, subjective, determined in large part by students' abilities to persuade my own train of thought with their argumentation and insight, this subjectivity compounded by the necessity of the journaling questions' open-endedness; however, my inclusion of this criterion allows me to discount or otherwise penalize responses deficient in terms of their legitimacy. Over the course of one novel's teaching unit, entries accumulate within the students' journals, ultimately symbolizing the readers' substantive engagement with and interpretation of the literature, far beyond what traditional reading quizzes allow.

Lists of potential questions for each of the novel's scenes are included below. Additionally, for "The Custom-House: Introductory to *The Scarlet Letter*," I have included an interpretive organizer on page 51 of the Chapter Materials section, which students might use to guide the reading and comprehension of this admittedly tricky introductory chapter.

- *"The Custom-House: Introductory to* The Scarlet Letter*"*: In the novel's introductory chapter, Hawthorne essentially establishes the narrative style that he uses throughout *The Scarlet Letter*, namely the combination of historical allusion, extremely observant sensory and emotional description, and a touch of the supernatural. How are all three of these components incorporated into this introductory chapter describing Hawthorne's employment history?

- *Chapter 1*: Throughout *The Scarlet Letter*, Hawthorne utilizes natural flora and fauna in symbolic ways; this tendency is of course immediately visible in the plot's first chapter. In fact, Hawthorne in Chapter 1 juxtaposes naturally growing life with the constructed outcomes of human labor; what is the figurative or otherwise meaningful effect in this chapter of the juxtaposition of the natural world with the man-made world?

- *Chapter 2*: Many critics interpret *The Scarlet Letter* as a proto-feminist work of literature; others read it contrarily, as an indictment of the female gender. We are introduced in Chapter 2 to Hester Prynne—an individual—and to other women of Puritan Boston. Based upon his descriptions of them in this chapter, how do you feel that Hawthorne represents or views women as the novel begins?

- *Chapter 3*: In contrast to the previous chapter, in Chapter 3, we are introduced to a variety of male citizens of Boston, including Mister Wilson and

Reverend Dimmesdale, as well as a mysterious stranger on the outskirts of the crowd. Based upon these initial portrayals of men in an admittedly male-dominated time and culture, what are *your* impressions of these persons? How do you respond to them, either emotionally or intellectually?

- *Chapter 4*: Made clear in Chapter 4 are the relationship between Hester Prynne and the man identified as Roger Chillingworth, as well as their motivations, apparent philosophies of justice, and individual desires. Based upon the characters' actions and interaction in this chapter, analyze all of these particular aspects of both persons.

- *Chapter 5*: From the eponymous scarlet letter itself to Hester's chosen profession, and from the clothing of the young child to the adornments of the society as a whole, Chapter 5 focuses much attention on the practices, products, and effects of sewing. How does Hawthorne in this chapter portray needlework as a craft, as well as the various wearers of its heterogeneous products?

- *Chapter 6*: Irony of various sorts—dramatic, verbal, and situational—surely arises in this chapter describing Hester Prynne's daughter Pearl. Where and how do these forms of irony exist in Chapter 6, and why in your estimation has Hawthorne chosen to include them here?

- *Chapter 7*: This chapter opens at some indistinct point "one day" in the future. Clearly events have occurred in the temporal space between Chapters 5 and 7, but Hawthorne as the story's architect chooses to jump in his plot to the Prynnes' visit to Governor Bellingham's mansion. What clues does he offer in Chapter 7 as to what may have transpired in the interim, and why in your estimation did he choose to pass them by in moving forward to this point?

- *Chapter 8*: We see the Prynnes in Chapter 8 interact with persons who are oppositional, if not outright foils, in several important ways: firstly the group composed of Governor Bellingham, Reverend Dimmesdale, and Mister Wilson, and secondly the mysterious Mistress Hibbins. What do these specific persons and groups apparently represent in both Hester's world and the larger world of Puritan New England, and why do you believe that Hawthorne chose to juxtapose their particular interactions with the Prynnes within this chapter?

- *Chapter 9*: From characters' names to actions to facial expressions, Chapter 9 is seemingly full of symbolic details. Where and how do you ascertain metaphor and other symbolic effects in the particulars of this chapter?

- *Chapter 10*: Among this chapter's narrative purposes is the establishment and/or enlargement of characterization. All four of the novel's major characters appear, and all four are emotionally or characteristically illuminated herein. In what ways do Hawthorne's portrayals of Hester, Pearl, Chillingworth, and Dimmesdale change within Chapter 10, and in what ways do they remain relatively unchanged?

- *Chapter 11*: One of the clearest themes in *The Scarlet Letter* concerns potential differences between people's interior truths and exterior appearances; stated plainly, what is seen is not always what is real. In what ways is this idea probed in Chapter 11, and based on Hawthorne's own diction and syntax in exploring the distinction, what do you infer his position on the issue to be?

- *Chapter 12*: Alongside several other tangible symbols, namely Hester's scarlet letter itself, the scaffold in Boston's town square exists in this novel as a physical metaphor, functioning on levels both pragmatic (i.e., as an actual, legally useable scaffold) and figurative. Based upon characters' interactions at the scaffold and Hawthorne's own description of it in Chapter 12, what symbolic connotations does it seem to be emitting or developing?

- *Chapter 13*: A dynamic character in any story is one who evolves emotionally or intellectually during the passage of the story's plot, in contrast to a relatively unchanged static character. Hester proves herself in Chapter 13 to be quite dynamic in this respect. How or why? Please compose a journal entry utilizing evidence both from this chapter and from previous portions of the novel to analyze Hester's interior development thus far.

- *Chapter 14*: The terms "good guy" and "bad guy" are commonly used, but necessarily malleable when it comes to literary criticism; antiheroes in various stories commonly transgress laws or other legitimate authorities, yet usually garner their readers' sympathies. Thus, deciphering which persons qualify as sympathetic figures in the eyes of a readership is perhaps a more accurate method of determining a given story's emotional impact. Chapter 14 of *The Scarlet Letter* is useful in this respect, allowing readers to gauge their own sympathies for all of the major, admittedly flawed, characters. Thus, based upon their interactions with one another in this chapter, with whom do you find yourself sympathizing in this novel?

- *Chapter 15*: Young Pearl is the central figure of Chapter 15, functioning as both an independent character to be analyzed and a narrative mechanism for eliciting responsive action from her mother. This duality of purpose is so true, in fact, that it is hard to know whether we should read her as an importantly individual person in this book or as a simple symbol, like Hester's scarlet letter or the prison rosebush. In your opinion, should we analyze Pearl just as we do her mother, Chillingworth, and Dimmesdale, or are we to see her solely as a mechanism for Hawthorne's communication of theme? Justify your answer with evidence from Chapter 15 and the rest of the novel thus far.

- *Chapter 16*: The distinction that Hawthorne makes between city and forest, between civilization and wilderness, owes much to his literary and historical predecessors' portrayals of and beliefs about the wild woods. That being said, his own juxtaposition of the forest and the city of Boston, and the resultant import of their contrast, is illuminated in Chapter 16. Based on evidence from this chapter, how do you believe that Hawthorne both views and utilizes these two different locales? What do they seemingly represent in the world of *The Scarlet Letter*?

- *Chapter 17*: Dimmesdale, in this chapter, assesses the value and result of his own life, choices, and effects; Hester does the same, although she reaches some different conclusions about the minister's person than he does himself. With which assessment of Dimmesdale—his own or Hester Prynne's—do you believe that Hawthorne wishes us to concur? Support your answer with evidence both from Chapter 17 and from elsewhere in the novel.

- *Chapter 18*: Entitled "A Flood of Sunshine," Chapter 18 focuses among other things on Hawthorne's symbolic use of light, shading, and darkness. In what ways, and to what effects, does Hawthorne make figurative use of light, or its absence, and is this interpretation valid in the novel elsewhere than in Chapter 18?

- *Chapter 19*: The sylvan brook by which characters interact in this chapter functions in several ways and accrues various importances both literal and figurative. To Hester, to Pearl, and to the insightful reader, what is the importance of the brook, both actually and symbolically, at this point of the novel? In what ways does the brook in this chapter actually move Hawthorne's thematic narrative forward?

- *Chapter 20*: Unlike at any other point of *The Scarlet Letter* thus far, Dimmesdale begins Chapter 20 feeling hopeful. Resultantly, his character actually changes here from what it has heretofore seemed to be. Perhaps Hawthorne intended, therefore, for this chapter to demonstrate something that he believed about hope as a human emotion or thought, as well as the effect of its presence on people's action. Where and how in this chapter do you see the impactful effect of hope on Dimmesdale's dynamic characterization?

- *Chapter 21*: Nathaniel Hawthorne is without doubt a skillful writer; his details, syntax, and diction evoke images, ideas, and emotions that few other writers can produce. Focus on his descriptions—physical, emotional, and intellectual—in this chapter. What in your estimation most clearly demonstrates his evocative ability and linguistic polish? In other words, where and how in Chapter 21 does Hawthorne demonstrate his dominance as a supremely talented writer?

- *Chapter 22*: The crowd in central Boston, as described in Chapter 22, is of course intended to recall for us the throng that gathered in that same place in the novel's earliest chapters, when Hester first emerged with her scarlet letter and her child. How has the mass of people, and potentially some individuals within it, changed since that earlier gathering, and what might this evolution demonstrate about what Hawthorne wishes us to view in retrospect of the story's events and characters?

- *Chapter 23*: In a climax of drama of symbolism, a number of conflicts of *The Scarlet Letter* reach their resolutions in this chapter, at the conclusion of which success is achieved and goals are reached by several characters. Which characters, then, do you judge to be victorious at the end of this penultimate chapter of the novel? In more simplistic terms, who seemingly has won, and who has lost?

- *Chapter 24*: This final chapter of *The Scarlet Letter* very much serves the purpose of a traditional epilogue, wrapping up loose ends from the tale and explaining what happens in time far beyond the plot's scope. In this sense, why might Hawthorne have made the ultimate choices that he did regarding his characters' outcomes? Why in your estimation did he choose for the novel's persons the final results and destinations that he did, and what might his choices demonstrate about how he hoped that his readership would ultimately view the story and its participants?

AP-Style Quizzes

The AP English Literature and Composition Exam's multiple-choice section requires students to read short passages of prose and poetry in order to answer questions that require precise comprehension and insightful analysis of the pieces' literary devices, purposes, tonal effects, themes, and formal structures. This portion of the test exerts upon students great pressure to manage time effectively, as it consistently includes approximately the same number of multiple-choice questions as it provides students with minutes in which to answer them (i.e., it usually entails answering 60 or so questions in 60 minutes). If a student were to spend one minute on each multiple choice question, then he or she would mathematically have no time left to read and decipher the literary selections themselves, which is of course necessary. Needless to say, this section of the test should not be approached cold by AP Literature students. To the contrary, students who practice on assessments mimicking the multiple-choice section's format and level of difficulty learn to develop time- and stress-management techniques, test-taking strategies, interpretive skills under pressure, a strong literary knowledge base, and overall greater comfort and confidence with the demands of the test.

Included at the end of this chapter are several different AP-style quizzes that I designed with this kind of mimicry (and thus test-taking payoff) in mind. These assessments are *not* traditional reading quizzes that evaluate students' understanding of assigned nightly homework, but instead pop quizzes intended to be administered at particular points of your class's progress through the plot. Suggested time limits for all quizzes are included, including one minute per question, plus just a minute or two during which to read each excerpt. Adherence to these suggested time limits should help students to develop level-headedness and time-management experience.

The AP-style quizzes are included at the end of this chapter, on pages 57–66, and answers to the quizzes' questions are included on page 67.

Quotation Analysis Quizzes and Activities

In today's technologically united Western world, it is an unfortunate fact of education that completing assigned reading for homework has become more avoidable than ever for savvy, intelligent students. I recently had a high school student of my own admit, upon matriculating to my course, that she had not actually read a book since the sixth grade. When I asked how she managed to earn her straight A grades, she simply replied, "SparkNotes." Now there is surely nothing wrong with students' usages of such synoptic resources to augment their readings of text, but the *replacement* of students' encounters with the actual literature itself is of course not what any English teacher desires.

Traditional reading quizzes asking and ascertaining students' knowledge of plot-based questions (e.g., "What is the setting?" and "Who is the antagonist?") allow, if not potentially encourage, such avoidance of the actual text. For students today, as forever, there remain only 24 hours in each day, yet students in the 21st century increasingly have to accrue extracurricular responsibilities and nonscholastic accomplishments in order to keep up in the ever-challenging race for college admissions. It is understandable why students might take the proverbial easy way and read synopses rather than literary chapters on any given night.

To prevent such shirking in my own classes, I administer quotation quizzes much like the ones found in the collected Chapter Materials at the end of this chapter, on pages 68–95. These quizzes require students to decipher the significances of various quotes from the novel, requiring not only their actual reading of the text itself, as opposed to basically outlined synopses, but also their close attention to and comprehension of it! Additionally, I utilize in my courses and here similarly include alternate forms of the reading quizzes for each section of text, which not only discourages students' cheating further, but also allows potential retakes. As opposed to multiple-choice AP-style quizzes, these instruments can be used following nightly reading assignments to assess comprehension and completion of homework. The inclusion of alternate quiz forms—A and B, respectively—allows you the option either to distribute them both throughout your room during an administration of a reading quiz or to institute a retake policy for your course, validly allowing students the opportunity to raise their grades on an alternate assessment.

Lesson Plan: Anachronistic Time Capsules

The activity in this lesson plan allows students to perform historical research and then use computerized technology in order to create and share with their classmates presentations concerning the two time periods of *The Scarlet Letter*. The assignment is framed in terms of the compilation of a cultural time capsule, the contents of which should represent everyday life for both Puritan and mid-19th century Massachusetts. Students' understanding of the novel's historical setting and the place and time of its author's life will thereby be strengthened.

The complete lesson plan for this activity is included on pages 52–56.

Conclusion

This chapter concludes with the reproducible pages for all of the AP-style quizzes and quotation analysis quizzes. The next chapter provides various activities for understanding at a deeper level the themes and artistry of *The Scarlet Letter*, helping students to move beyond basic plot and style comprehension into a fuller experience with the novel as a philosophical, thematically meaningful work.

Chapter Materials

Name: _____ Date: _____

Vocabulary Analysis Sheet

Sentence or clause in which the vocabulary word is used:

_____
_____
_____
_____
_____
_____

Importance / meaning of this sentence at this point of the novel:

Chapter and page of sentence:

Prefix:

Definition:

Root:

Vocabulary Word:

Part of Speech:

Suffix:

Synonyms:

Judgment: Why did Hawthorne choose to use this particular word in this case?

Name: _____ Date: _____

"The Custom-House" Organizer

According to "The Custom-House," how did Nathaniel Hawthorne feel or think about things?

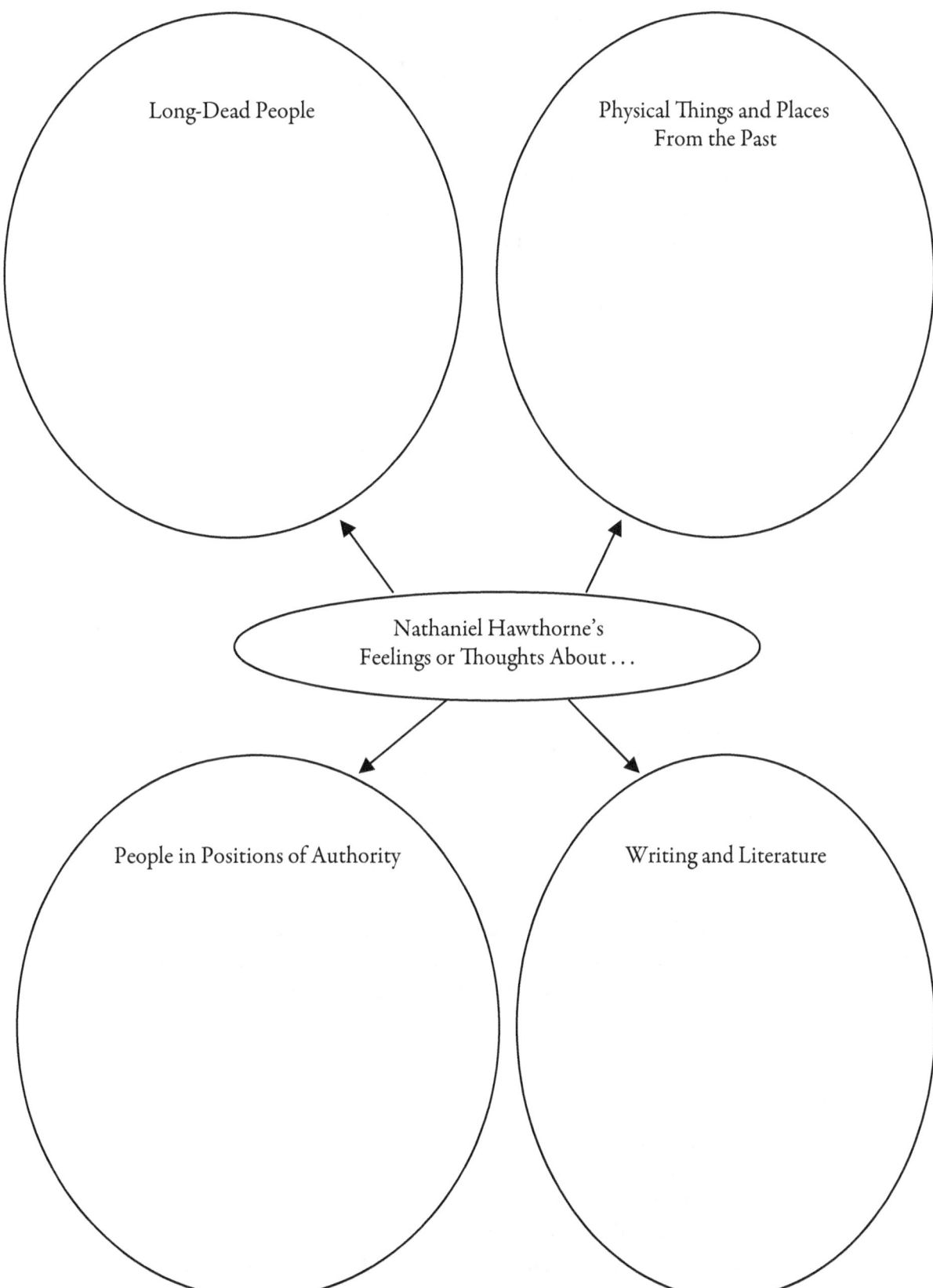

Reading The Scarlet Letter   51

LESSON 1

Lesson Plan:
Anachronistic Time Capsules

Purpose/Objective

This activity is designed to help students research and understand several differences between the setting of *The Scarlet Letter* in Puritan Boston and the place and time of its composition, mid-19th century Massachusetts. Students will develop their research and presentation skills, as well as their note-taking abilities, and will strengthen their understanding of Hawthorne's and Hester Prynne's distinct cultures.

Placement

This lesson should be completed prior to beginning your students' reading of *The Scarlet Letter*, as it both anticipates several aspects of "The Custom-House: Introductory to *The Scarlet Letter*" chapter and will aid their later visualization and comprehension of the story's central plot itself.

Materials Required

For the research component of this lesson, you will require either hard copy resources, such as encyclopedias or textbooks concerning social mores and cultural trends of the appropriate time periods, or computers enabled with Internet access, allowing students to conduct online research. For the presentation portion of the lesson, you will require computers loaded with design and presentation software, such as Microsoft Powerpoint.

Duration

If completed fully in class, this activity should occur over three approximately one-hour class periods. If all preparatory work is completed outside of class, then the presentations alone should occur over one approximately one-hour class period.

Lesson Plan

1. *Anticipatory Set:* Ask students to answer the following question in their notebooks: If you were to construct a time capsule, the purpose of which is to inform future generations of what everyday life is like for all of us today, then what kinds of things would you include in it? After they consider the question and compose, have them pair and share their answers with

one another, then ask for volunteers to share aloud with the class. This question may inspire answers that allow you to pigeonhole artifacts into cultural genres or categories, such as pastimes, fashion, technology, and education.

2. *Communication of Objective:* After discussing what students' ideas for the time capsule are, discuss the ways in which cultural artifacts generally communicate more about the major citizenry of a given time and place than academic textbooks and the like do; after all, most social studies texts that your students have experienced discuss military histories, political evolutions, and the lives of various ruling classes, rather than the "rank and file" people who constitute the world's majority. Informing them that *The Scarlet Letter* is a work of historical fiction, and that it would have been classified as such even at the time of its initial publication because its literary setting was 200 years prior to its publication date, describe how an understanding of the daily lives of people in both Puritan Boston and 19th century Massachusetts will enhance their understanding and enjoyment of the novel. That fuller understanding and enjoyment, of course, is the goal of the lesson, which will require them to research, gather, and present to each other artifacts that retrospectively might serve the same "time capsule" function as the objects about which they just brainstormed.

3. *Division of Labor:* You will need students or groups of students who are responsible for investigating and making choices about 12 distinct cultural areas of research, namely each of the following categories relative both to Puritan Massachusetts and to mid-19th century Massachusetts: education, literacy, and the cultural arts; everyday technologies; fashions for men, women, and children; architecture, urban development, and transportation; political issues, parties, and beliefs; and popular pastimes and entertainments. Thus, please divide your class into 12 such groups.

4. *Research and Artifact Gathering:* If you wish to accomplish this portion of the lesson in class, then allow your students approximately one hour to research their respective areas of responsibility, focusing on two major tasks: a "big picture" understanding of their own cultural category for the assigned time period and several separate choices of "time capsule artifacts" that strongly represent that category. You might offer as an example the choices of a smartphone, a remote control, and a sketchbook to represent common pastimes of teenagers living today. Your students should investigate their areas of responsibility, ultimately choosing several such representative artifacts. This portion of the lesson may also be accomplished for homework.

5. *Organization:* After students gather their findings, they need to organize them into a presentable format. You may wish to require that their

individual presentations include not only an overview of their particular cultural area of responsibility for the given time period, but also three distinct objects—including pictures—that represent it best. Presentation software such as Microsoft Powerpoint or Prezi enables such organizational work well, but old-fashioned resources such as poster board and glue sticks can do just as well. Overall, though, students may need approximately one hour to complete a decent production, which likewise can be accomplished for homework.

6. *Presentations:* The final portion of this activity of course requires that students present their findings and choices to one another. Reproducible pages are included here, on which your students can take and organize notes during the series of presentations. You may wish to require successful completion of these graphic organizers/note sheets for a final grade, in addition to the students' individual presentations to the class.

Closure

You may wish to have your students conflate all of their findings and understandings into a larger de facto research essay comparing and/or contrasting the two time periods. Resources for assigning, collecting, and grading essays of various sorts can be found in Chapter 6: Writing About *The Scarlet Letter*, found on pages 143–181.

Name: _____ Date: _____

Cultural Norms in Puritan Massachusetts

- Technologies Used Every Day
- Fashions for Children and Adults
- Architecture, Urban Development, and Transportation
- Education, Literacy, and Cultural Arts
- Pastimes and Entertainments
- Political Issues and Common Political Beliefs

Boston
Massachusetts Bay Colony
Approximately 1645

Reading The Scarlet Letter 55

Cultural Norms in Mid-19th Century Massachusetts

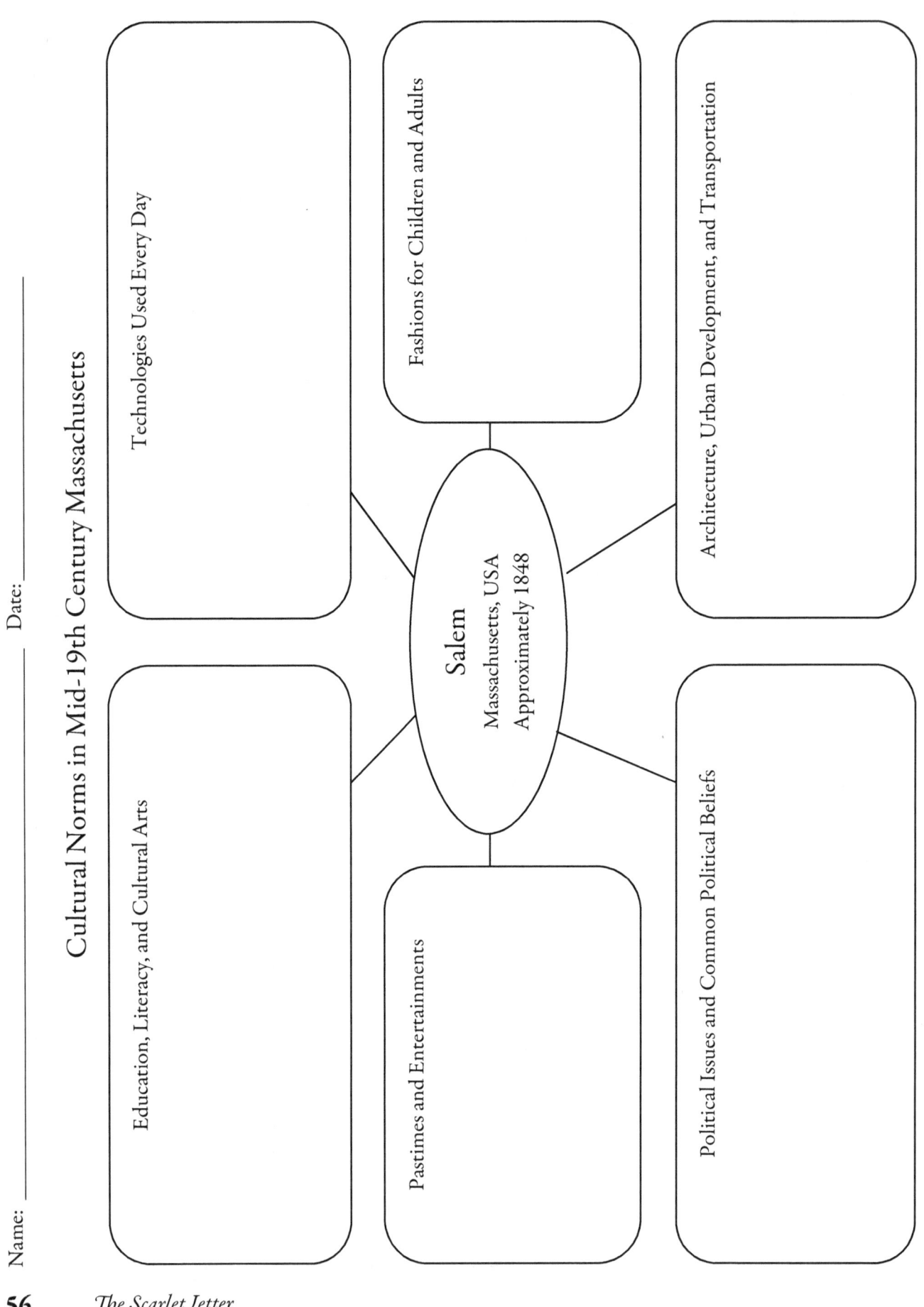

Name: _____ Date: _____

AP-Style Multiple Choice Quiz
The Scarlet Letter, "The Custom-House"

Directions: This quiz consists of a selection from the introductory chapter "The Custom-House" and questions regarding its content, form, and style. After reading the excerpt, choose and circle the best answer to each question.

Read the following excerpt carefully before choosing your answers. **Suggested time: 9 minutes.**

    In my native town of Salem, at the head of what, half a century ago, in the days of old King Derby, was a bustling wharf,—but which is now burdened with decayed wooden warehouses, and exhibits few or no symptoms of commercial life; except, perhaps, a bark or brig, half-way down its melancholy length, discharging hides; or, nearer at hand, a Nova Scotia
5 schooner, pitching out her cargo of fire-wood,—at the head, I say, of this dilapidated wharf, which the tide often overflows, and along which, at the base and in the rear of the row of buildings, the track of many languid years is seen in a border of unthrifty grass,—here, with a view from its front windows adown this not very enlivening prospect, and thence across the harbor, stands a spacious edifice of brick. From the loftiest point of its roof, during precisely
10 three and a half hours of each forenoon, floats or droops, in breeze or calm, the banner of the republic; but with the thirteen stripes turned vertically, instead of horizontally, and thus indicating that a civil, and not a military post of Uncle Sam's government, is here established. Its front is ornamented with a portico of half a dozen wooden pillars, supporting a balcony, beneath which a flight of wide granite steps descends towards the street. Over the entrance hovers an enormous
15 specimen of the American eagle, with outspread wings, a shield before her breast, and, if I recollect aright, a bunch of intermingled thunder-bolts and barbed arrows in each claw. With the customary infirmity of temper that characterizes this unhappy fowl, she appears, by the fierceness of her beak and eye, and the general truculency of her attitude, to threaten mischief to the inoffensive community; and especially to warn all citizens, careful of their safety, against
20 intruding on the premises which she overshadows with her wings. Nevertheless, vixenly as she looks, many people are seeking, at this very moment, to shelter themselves under the wing of the federal eagle; imagining, I presume, that her bosom has all the softness and snugness of an eider-down pillow. But she has no great tenderness, even in her best of moods, and, sooner or later,—oftener soon than late,—is apt to fling off her nestlings, with a scratch of her claw, a dab of her
25 beak, or a rankling wound from her barbed arrows.

1. The purpose of the excerpt's first sentence (lines 1–9) is to
   (A) describe the United States' political culture in the 19th century
   (B) portray King Derby as an important contemporary of the author
   (C) isolate the town of Salem's moral character near its harbor
   (D) characterize Salem's wharf as archaic and decaying
   (E) describe the abundance of foreign immigrants in Salem

2. Line 9 of the excerpt includes diction that introduces
   (A) a sudden shift in descriptive tone
   (B) a dilapidated, once-powerful city and harbor
   (C) an unusually emphatic reliance on punctuation
   (D) the narrator's expressed desire for governmental work
   (E) a change in setting both physical and temporal

Name: _____ Date: _____

3. Hawthorne's reference to Uncle Sam on line 12 is an example of
    (A) metonymy
    (B) hyperbole
    (C) imagery
    (D) caesura
    (E) allegory

4. The description of the governmental building in lines 9–16 emphasizes
    (A) that the building is older than anything else in Salem
    (B) the degree to which the building is ornamentally colored
    (C) particular diction indicating languidness and inactivity
    (D) the attitude of Salem towards its chief military outpost
    (E) the building's height relative to the rest of the wharf

5. Hawthorne's description of the American eagle in lines 14–25 symbolically portrays
    (A) the narrator himself as a servant of old King Derby
    (B) the United States Government as supercilious and vengeful
    (C) the citizenry of Salem as watchfully ready for war
    (D) Salem's wharf as inactive and past its economic prime
    (E) a paradoxical statement of cowardice and courage

6. Hawthorne's description of the American eagle as a female (lines 14–25) might be labeled
    (A) humanistic hyperbole
    (B) redundantly metaphoric
    (C) misogynistic personification
    (D) unnecessarily isolating
    (E) anachronistically archaic

7. This excerpt's overall description of the "spacious edifice of brick" (line 9) is largely
    (A) satirical
    (B) directive
    (C) immaterial
    (D) metonymic
    (E) imaginary

The Scarlet Letter

Name: _____   Date: _____

AP-Style Multiple Choice Quiz
The Scarlet Letter, Chapters I–VI

Directions: This quiz consists of a selection from the first six chapters of *The Scarlet Letter* and questions regarding its content, form, and style. After reading the excerpt, choose and circle the best answer to each question.

Read the following excerpt carefully before choosing your answers. **Suggested time: 9 minutes.**

Certainly, there was no physical defect. By its perfect shape, its vigor, and its natural dexterity in the use of all its untried limbs, the infant was worthy to have been brought forth in Eden; worthy to have been left there, to be the plaything of the angels, after the world's first parents were driven out. The child had a native grace which does not invariably coexist with
5   faultless beauty; its attire, however simple, always impressed the beholder as if it were the very garb that precisely became it best. But little Pearl was not clad in rustic weeds. Her mother, with a morbid purpose that may be better understood hereafter, had bought the richest tissues that could be procured, and allowed her imaginative faculty its full play in the arrangement and decoration of the dresses which the child wore, before the public eye. So magnificent was the
10   small figure, when thus arrayed, and such was the splendor of Pearl's own proper beauty, whining through the gorgeous robes which might have extinguished a paler loveliness, that there was an absolute circle of radiance around her, on the darksome cottage floor. And yet a russet gown, torn and soiled with the child's rude play, made a picture of her just as perfect. Pearl's aspect was imbued with a spell of infinite variety; in this one child there were many children,
15   comprehending the full scope between the wild-flower prettiness of a peasant-baby, and the pomp, in little, of an infant princess. Throughout all, however, there was a trait of passion, a certain depth of hue, which she never lost; and if, in any of her changes, she had grown fainter or paler, she would have ceased to be herself;—it would have been no longer Pearl!
    This outward mutability indicated, and did not more than fairly express, the various
20   properties of her inner life. Her nature appeared to possess depth, too, as well as variety; but—or else Hester's fear deceived her—it lacked reference and adaptation to the world into which she was born. The child could not be made amenable to rules. In giving her existence, a great law had been broken; and the result was a being whose elements were perhaps beautiful and brilliant, but all in disorder; or with an order peculiar to themselves, amidst which the point of variety and
25   arrangement was difficult or impossible to be discovered. Hester could only account for the child's character—and even then most vaguely and imperfectly—by recalling what she herself had been, during that momentous period while Pearl was imbibing her soul from the spiritual world, and her bodily frame from its material of earth. The mother's impassioned state had been the medium through which were transmitted to the unborn infant the rays of its moral life; and,
30   however white and clear originally, they had taken the deep stains of crimson and gold, the fiery luster, the black shadow, and the untempered light, of the intervening substance.

1. Line 3 of this excerpt contains
   (A) a Biblical allusion
   (B) a comparative simile
   (C) descriptive imagery
   (D) an interior monologue
   (E) first person narration

Name: _____ Date: _____

2. In lines 1–9, Hawthorne makes a point of juxtaposing
   (A) the distance of heavenly bodies with the immediacy of Earth-grown weeds
   (B) the child's physical dexterity with its mother's sedentary imaginativeness
   (C) the perfection of the heavens with the flawed extravagance of humans
   (D) spiritual worlds of the church with secular worlds of artistic creativity
   (E) coexistent traits that metaphorically indicate Pearl's own mortality

3. In lines 11–18, Hawthorne connotatively associates strength and weakness respectively with
   (A) dirt and flowers
   (B) Pearl and her mother
   (C) openness and shelter
   (D) magic and naturalness
   (E) bright color and paleness

4. The purpose of lines 22–25 is largely to
   (A) establish the child's inhumanity
   (B) portray the child as dirty and ragged
   (C) communicate the child's unorthodox wildness
   (D) broach the topic of faith as a natural correlate of sin
   (E) describe the child's inherent lawfulness and kind character

5. It becomes clear by the end of the selection that
   (A) Hester believes herself to be somewhat culpable for Pearl's character
   (B) townspeople look down upon young Pearl as an ostentatious child
   (C) Hester's desire to dress her child in rags has produced a social effect
   (D) Pearl is herself entirely in control of her own emotions and decisions
   (E) Pearl is adaptable to stimuli from various persons and situations

6. Hawthorne creates a foreboding emotional effect at the end of the selection by
   (A) juxtaposing whiteness and clearness with color and brightness
   (B) describing Pearl's moral character as unaccountably pure
   (C) utilizing diction that recalls shallowness and lightness
   (D) relying upon straightforward language free of metaphor and imagery
   (E) suggesting that Pearl's future will be religiously volatile

Name: _____ Date: _____

AP-Style Multiple Choice Quiz
The Scarlet Letter, Chapters VII–XII

Directions: This quiz consists of a selection from Chapters 7–12 of *The Scarlet Letter* and questions regarding its content, form, and style. After reading the excerpt, choose and circle the best answer to each question.

Read the following excerpt carefully before choosing your answers. **Suggested time: 8 minutes.**

The old minister seated himself in an arm-chair, and made an effort to draw Pearl betwixt his knees. But the child, unaccustomed to the touch or familiarity of any but her mother, escaped through the open window, and stood on the upper step, looking like a wild tropical bird, of rich plumage, ready to take flight into the upper air. Mr. Wilson, not a little astonished at this
5 outbreak,—for he was a grandfatherly sort of personage, and usually a vast favorite with children, —essayed, however, to proceed with the examination.
"Pearl," said he, with great solemnity, "thou must take heed to instruction, that so, in due season, thou mayest wear in thy bosom the pearl of great price. Canst thou tell me, my child, who made thee?"
10 Now Pearl knew well enough who made her; for Hester Prynne, the daughter of a pious home, very soon after her talk with the child about her Heavenly Father, had begun to inform her of those truths which the human spirit, at whatever stage of immaturity, imbibes with such eager interest. Pearl, therefore, so large were the attainments of her three years' lifetime, could have borne a fair examination in the New England Primer, or the first column of the Westminster
15 Catechisms, although unacquainted with the outward form of either of those celebrated works. But that perversity, which all children have more or less of, and of which little Pearl had a tenfold portion, now, at the most inopportune moment, took thorough possession of her, and closed her lips, or impelled her to speak words amiss. After putting her finger in her mouth, with many ungracious refusals to answer good Mr. Wilson's question, the child finally announced that she
20 had not been made at all, but had been plucked by her mother off the bush of wild roses that grew by the prison-door.
This fantasy was probably suggested by the near proximity of the Governor's red roses, as Pearl stood outside of the window; together with her recollection of the prison rose-bush, which she had passed in coming hither.

1. The opening of this excerpt associates
   (A) old age with stillness and youth with flight
   (B) freedom with touch and anxiety with air
   (C) furniture with confinement and children with religion
   (D) mothers with strangeness and grandfathers with familiarity
   (E) instruction with improvement and creation with custom

2. Hawthorne's description on lines 10–11 of "Hester Prynne [as] the daughter of a pious home" is
   (A) hyperbolized
   (B) coincidental
   (C) irrelevant
   (D) ironic
   (E) false

Name: _____ Date: _____

3. Lines 13–15 are important in indicating Pearl's
   (A) inability
   (B) happiness
   (C) precociousness
   (D) destructiveness
   (E) social introversion

4. The child Pearl is at several points in this chapter figuratively associated with
   (A) the humanly created world of buildings
   (B) the natural world of animals and plants
   (C) her mother's completely solitary world
   (D) the minister's world of age and wisdom
   (E) an unnatural world of prevented spontaneity

5. The overall narrative goal of this selection seems to be
   (A) a depiction of Mr. Wilson's living quarters
   (B) a portrayal of Hester as ashamed
   (C) a characterization of Pearl
   (D) an unusual depiction of religion as aviary
   (E) a description of the nearby rosebush

6. It is clear from this selection that Mr. Wilson is all of the following except
   (A) solemn
   (B) a minister
   (C) the Governor
   (D) religious
   (E) elderly

Name: _____ Date: _____

AP-Style Multiple Choice Quiz
The Scarlet Letter, Chapters XIII–XVIII

Directions: This quiz consists of a selection from Chapters 13–18 of *The Scarlet Letter* and questions regarding its content, form, and style. After reading the excerpt, choose and circle the best answer to each question.

Read the following excerpt carefully before choosing your answers. **Suggested time: 8 minutes.**

   All this while, Hester had been looking steadily at the old man, and was shocked, as well as wonder-smitten, to discern what a change had been wrought upon him within the past seven years. It was not so much that he had grown older; for though the traces of advancing life were visible, he bore his age well, and seemed to retain a wiry vigor and alertness. But the former
5 aspect of an intellectual and studious man, calm and quiet, which was what she best remembered in him, had altogether vanished, and been succeeded by an eager, searching, almost fierce, yet carefully guarded look. It seemed to be his wish and purpose to mask this expression with a smile; but the latter played him false, and flickered over his visage so derisively, that the spectator could see his blackness all the better for it. Ever and anon, too, there came a glare of red light out
10 of his eyes; as if the old man's soul were on fire, and kept on smouldering duskily within his breast, until, by some casual puff of passion, it was blown into a momentary flame. This he repressed, as speedily as possible, and strove to look as if nothing of the kind had happened.
   In a word, Roger Chillingworth was a striking evidence of man's faculty of transforming himself into a devil, if he will only, for a reasonable space of time, undertake a devil's office.
15 This unhappy person had effected such a transformation, by devoting himself, for seven years, to the constant analysis of a heart full of torture, and deriving his enjoyment thence, and adding fuel to those fiery tortures which he analyzed and gloated over.
   The scarlet letter burned on Hester Prynne's bosom. Here was another ruin, the responsibility of which came partly home to her.
20 "What see you in my face," asked the physician, "that you look at it so earnestly?"
   "Something that would make me weep, if there were any tears bitter enough for it," answered she.

1. One effect of Hawthorne's syntactical choices in lines 1–7 is
   (A) a portrayal of Hester Prynne and Roger Chillingworth as equally devilish characters
   (B) a view of Roger Chillingworth from Hester's observant perspective
   (C) the appropriate utilization of the second person narrative point of view
   (D) the usage of metaphor to describe Roger Chillingworth's character
   (E) an unsettling departure from accepted grammatical practices

2. Roger Chillingworth is characterized both directly and indirectly in lines 6–9 through
   (A) carefully placed punctuation
   (B) descriptive personification
   (C) consideration of the future
   (D) strongly connotative diction
   (E) religious allusions

3. Lines 13–14 seem to encapsulate
   (A) a cautionary theme
   (B) Hester's moral inferiority
   (C) the excerpt's temporal setting
   (D) an argument against cosmic justice
   (E) a portrayal of the narrator's emotions

4. Hawthorne on lines 9–11 repeatedly associates
   (A) breath with mortal death
   (B) flame with personal ability
   (C) Roger Chillingworth with fire
   (D) motivated action with freedom
   (E) dark colors with impermanence

5. It is implied on lines 18–19 that Hester Prynne and Roger Chillingworth
   (A) are similar characters
   (B) care nothing for each other
   (C) will share an eventual destiny
   (D) are culpable in the eyes of the law
   (E) are ethically accountable to one another

6. This excerpt utilizes all of the following descriptive techniques except
   (A) dialogue
   (B) imagery
   (C) metaphor
   (D) parody
   (E) connotation

Name: _____ Date: _____

AP-Style Multiple Choice Quiz
The Scarlet Letter, Chapters XIX–XXIV

Directions: This quiz consists of a selection from the final six chapters of *The Scarlet Letter* and questions regarding its content, form, and style. After reading the excerpt, choose and circle the best answer to each question.

Read the following excerpt carefully before choosing your answers. **Suggested time: 8 minutes.**

   Nothing was more remarkable than the change which took place, almost immediately after Mr. Dimmesdale's death, in the appearance and demeanor of the old man known as Roger Chillingworth. All his strength and energy—all his vital and intellectual force—seemed at once to desert him; insomuch that he positively withered up, shrivelled away, and almost vanished
5 from mortal sight, like an uprooted weed that lies wilting in the sun. This unhappy man had made the very principle of his life to consist in the pursuit and systematic exercise of revenge; and when, by its completest triumph and consummation, that evil principle was left with no further material to support it, when, in short, there was no more Devil's work on earth for him to do, it only remained for the unhumanized mortal to betake himself whither his Master would find him
10 tasks enough, and pay him his wages duly. But, to all these shadowy beings, so long our near acquaintances,—as well Roger Chillingworth as his companions,—we would fain be merciful. It is a curious subject of observation and inquiry, whether hatred and love be not the same thing at bottom. Each, in its utmost development, supposes a high degree of intimacy and heart-knowledge; each renders one individual dependent for the food of his affections and spiritual life
15 upon another; each leaves the passionate lover, or the no less passionate hater, forlorn and desolate by the withdrawal of his subject. Philosophically considered, therefore, the two passions seem essentially the same, except that one happens to be seen in a celestial radiance, and the other in a dusky and lurid glow. In the spiritual world, the old physician and the minister—mutual victims as they have been—may, unawares, have found their earthly stock of hatred and antipathy
20 transmuted into golden love.

1. Hawthorne's third person narration of Chillingworth's final transformation relies upon
   (A) omniscient descriptions of characters' dynamic emotions
   (B) the associative usage of first person narrative pronouns
   (C) neither figurative language nor philosophical theory
   (D) both physical description and intellectual conjecture
   (E) the reader's foreknowledge of characters' pasts

2. Hawthorne's reference on line 9 to Chillingworth's "Master" is
   (A) arbitrary syntax
   (B) allusive deification
   (C) unintended hyperbole
   (D) implied apostrophe
   (E) chiastic parellelism

3. Hawthorne describes the end of Chillingworth's life by utilizing a simile which
   (A) is split between this excerpt's beginning and end
   (B) states that he has perhaps found posthumous love
   (C) explicitly equates hatred with death
   (D) describes him in terms of an uprooted weed
   (E) theorizes that revenge requires sustenance

Reading The Scarlet Letter **65**

Name: _____ Date: _____

4. The words "shadowy" (ln. 10) and "dusky" (ln. 18) are here connotative of
   (A) furtiveness
   (B) brightness
   (C) humanness
   (D) immortality
   (E) immutability

5. The pronoun "each," as found on lines 13–15, refers to
   (A) the Devil and Chillingworth's Master
   (B) hatred and love
   (C) revenge and forgiveness
   (D) affection and passion
   (E) Chillingworth and Dimmesdale

6. Hawthorne concludes this excerpt somewhat hopefully through the usage of
   (A) interior monologue
   (B) hyperbolized caricature
   (C) a hypothesis concerning the afterlife
   (D) a description of the human mind
   (E) introspective memories

Multiple-Choice Quiz Answers

"The Custom-House"
1. D.
2. A.
3. A.
4. E.
5. B.
6. C.
7. A.

Chapters I–VI
1. A.
2. C.
3. E.
4. C.
5. A.
6. A.

Chapters VII–XII
1. A.
2. D.
3. C.
4. B.
5. C.
6. C.

Chapters XIII–XVIII
1. B.
2. D.
3. A.
4. C.
5. A.
6. D.

Chapters XIX–XXIV
1. D.
2. B.
3. D.
4. A.
5. B.
6. C.

Name: _____ Date: _____

"The Custom-House" Reading Quiz A

Directions: Below you see several quotations from the novel's introductory chapter. Please answer each question following the quotations as correctly and thoroughly as possible.

"What is he? . . . A writer of story-books! What kind of a business in life,—what mode of glorifying God, or being serviceable to mankind in his day and generation,—may that be? Why, the degenerate fellow might as well have been a fiddler!"

1. Who speaks these sentences?

   _____
   _____
   _____
   _____
   _____
   _____
   _____

2. Who is the "he" about whom these sentences are spoken?

   _____
   _____
   _____
   _____
   _____
   _____
   _____

"I happened to place it on my breast. It seemed to me,—the reader may smile, but must not doubt my word,—it seemed to me, then, that I experienced a sensation not altogether physical, yet almost so, as of burning heat . . ."

3. What is the "it" that Hawthorne describes here?

   _____
   _____
   _____
   _____
   _____
   _____
   _____

Name: _____ Date: _____

4. Where (i.e., in what physical space) did Hawthorne experience this "sensation … of burning heat"?

_____
_____
_____
_____
_____
_____

"The moment when a man's head drops off is seldom or never, I am inclined to think, precisely the most agreeable of his life. Nevertheless, like the greater part of our mis-fortunes, even so serious a contingency brings its remedy and consolation with it, if the sufferer will but make the best, rather than the worst, of the accident which has befallen him."

5. What is meant here by "a man's head drop[ping] off"?

_____
_____
_____
_____
_____
_____

6. How is Hawthorne referring to his own behavior in the last sentence of this quotation?

_____
_____
_____
_____
_____
_____

Reading The Scarlet Letter

Name: _____ Date: _____

"The Custom-House" Reading Quiz B

Directions: Below you see several quotations from the novel's introductory chapter. Please answer each question following the quotations as correctly and thoroughly as possible. Good luck!

"It is a good lesson—though it may often be a hard one—for a man who has dreamed of [*&*] fame, and of making for himself a rank among the world's dignitaries by such means, to step aside out of the narrow circle in which his claims are recognized, and to find how utterly devoid of significance, beyond that circle, is all that he achieves. I know not that I especially needed the lesson . . . but, at any rate, I learned it thoroughly . . ."

1. What kind of "fame" did Hawthorne particularly dream of (i.e., what sort of word or phrase has been cut from this quote at point [*&*] above)?

   _____
   _____
   _____
   _____
   _____
   _____
   _____

2. Where and by what means (i.e., how) did Hawthorne learn "the lesson" here described?

   _____
   _____
   _____
   _____
   _____
   _____
   _____

"Do this . . . do this, and the profit shall be all your own! You will shortly need it; for it is not in your days as it was in mine, when a man's office was a life-lease, and oftentimes an heirloom. But, I charge you, in this matter of old Mistress Prynne, give to your predecessor's memory the credit which will be rightfully due!"

3. Who speaks these sentences?

   _____
   _____
   _____
   _____
   _____
   _____
   _____

Name: _____ Date: _____

4. What exactly does the speaker of these sentences want the person to whom he is speaking to do (i.e., what is the charge here)?

_____
_____
_____
_____
_____
_____

"Meanwhile the press had taken up my affair, and kept me, for a week or two, careering through the public prints, in my decapitated state, like Irving's Headless Horseman; ghastly and grim, and longing to be buried . . . So much for my figurative self. The real human being, all this time, with his head safely on his shoulders, had brought himself to the comfortable conclusion that everything was for the best . . ."

5. What does Hawthorne mean by describing himself as a "decapitated . . . Headless Horseman"?

_____
_____
_____
_____
_____
_____

6. In what way (i.e., how and why) had he reached the "conclusion that everything was for the best"?

_____
_____
_____
_____
_____
_____

Reading The Scarlet Letter

Name: _____ Date: _____

The Scarlet Letter, Chapters 1–4 Reading Quiz A

Directions: Below you see several quotations from Chapters 1–4. Please answer each question following the quotations as correctly and thoroughly as possible.

"The founders of a new colony, whatever Utopia of human virtue and happiness they might originally project, have invariably recognized it among the earliest practical necessities to allot a portion of the virgin soil as a cemetery, and another portion as the site of..."

1. In the novel, how is this sentence concluded? (*Not necessarily the exact word(s), just the idea.*)

"...believe me, Hester, though he were to step down from a high place, and stand there beside thee, on thy pedestal of shame, yet better were it so, than to hide a guilty heart through life. What can thy silence do for him, except it tempt him—yea, compel him, as it were—to add hypocrisy to sin?"

2. Who speaks these sentences?

3. Where is the speaker of these sentences located when he or she speaks them?

Name: _____ Date: _____

"Recognize me not, by word, by sign, by look! Breathe not the secret, above all, to the man thou wottest of. Shouldst thou fail me in this, beware! His fame, his position, his life, will be in my hands. Beware!"

4. The person who speaks these sentences has at this point told people that his or her name is . . .

   _____
   _____
   _____
   _____
   _____
   _____
   _____

5. The speaker of these sentences is talking to Hester Prynne; in what physical space do they converse?

   _____
   _____
   _____
   _____
   _____
   _____
   _____

Reading The Scarlet Letter

Name: _____ Date: _____

The Scarlet Letter, Chapters 1–4 Reading Quiz B

Directions: Below you see several quotations from Chapters 1–4. Please answer each question following the quotations as correctly and thoroughly as possible.

"The founders of a new colony, whatever Utopia of human virtue and happiness they might originally project, have invariably recognized it among the earliest practical necessities to allot a portion of the virgin soil as a cemetery, and another portion as the site of . . ."

1. In the novel, how is this sentence concluded? (*Not necessarily the exact word(s), just the idea.*)

   _____
   _____
   _____
   _____
   _____
   _____
   _____

"'She will not speak!' murmured [he] . . . He now drew back, with a long respiration. 'Wondrous strength and generosity of a woman's heart! She will not speak!'"

2. Who is the "he" who speaks these sentences?

   _____
   _____
   _____
   _____
   _____
   _____
   _____

3. What exactly will "she . . . not speak"?

   _____
   _____
   _____
   _____
   _____
   _____
   _____

Name: _____ Date: _____

"Here, on this wild outskirt of the earth, I shall pitch my tent; for, elsewhere a wanderer, and isolated from human interests, I find here a woman, a man, a child, amongst whom and myself there exist the closest ligaments. No matter whether of love or hate; no matter whether of right or wrong!"

4. The person who speaks these sentences has at this point told others that his or her name is . . .

   _____
   _____
   _____
   _____
   _____
   _____

5. To whom is the speaker of these sentences talking, and where (i.e., in what physical space)?

   _____
   _____
   _____
   _____
   _____
   _____

Name: _____   Date: _____

The Scarlet Letter, Chapters 5–8 Reading Quiz A

Directions: Below you see several quotations from Chapters 5–8. Please answer each question following the quotations as correctly and thoroughly as possible.

"What evil thing is at hand? . . . Behold, Hester, here is a companion!"

1. Who speaks these sentences to Hester Prynne?

   _____
   _____
   _____
   _____
   _____
   _____
   _____

2. What is the significance of both of these sentences (i.e., what do they indicate or imply in the novel)?

   _____
   _____
   _____
   _____
   _____
   _____
   _____

"Brooding over all these matters, the mother felt like one who has evoked a spirit, but, by some irregularity in the process of conjuration, has failed to win the master-word that should control this new and incomprehensible intelligence."

3. What is the significance of this sentence (i.e., what "mother," what "spirit," what "new and incomprehensible intelligence" is Hawthorne describing here)?

   _____
   _____
   _____
   _____
   _____
   _____
   _____

Name: _____ Date: _____

"Among those who promoted the design, Governor Bellingham was said to be one of the most busy. It may appear singular, and indeed not a little ludicrous, that an affair of this kind, which, in later days, would have been referred to no higher jurisdiction that that of the selectmen of the town, should then have been a question publicly discussed, and on which statesmen of eminence took sides."

4. What "design," what "affair of this kind," is described here as important to Governor Bellingham?

_____
_____
_____
_____
_____
_____

"Behold, verily, there is the woman of the scarlet letter; and, of a truth, moreover, there is the likeness of the scarlet letter running along by her side! Come, therefore, and let us fling mud at them!"

5. Who speaks these sentences?

_____
_____
_____
_____
_____
_____

Reading The Scarlet Letter

The Scarlet Letter, Chapters 5–8 Reading Quiz B

Directions: Below you see several quotations from Chapters 5–8. Please answer each question following the quotations as correctly and thoroughly as possible. Good luck!

"The spell of life went forth from her ever creative spirit, and communicated itself to a thousand objects, as a torch kindles a flame wherever it may be applied. The unlikeliest materials,—a stick, a bunch of rags, a flower,—were the puppets of . . . witchcraft, and, without undergoing any outward change, became spiritually adapted to whatever drama occupied the stage of her inner world."

1. Who is the "her" here described?

"It was meant for a blessing; for the one blessing of her life! It was meant, doubtless, as the mother herself has told us, for a retribution too; a torture to be felt at many an unthought of moment; a pang, a sting, an ever-recurring agony, in the midst of a troubled joy!"

2. Who speaks these sentences?

3. What is the topic described (i.e., the "It" also described as "a torture")?

Name: _____ Date: _____

"Whenever that look appeared in her wild, bright, deeply black eyes, it invested her with a strange remoteness and intangibility; it was as if she were hovering in the air and might vanish, like a glimmering light, that comes we know not whence, and goes we know not whither."

4. Who is the "her" described by this sentence?

_____
_____
_____
_____
_____
_____

"Behold, verily, there is the woman of the scarlet letter; and, of a truth, moreover, there is the likeness of the scarlet letter running along by her side! Come, therefore, and let us fling mud at them!"

5. Who speaks these sentences?

_____
_____
_____
_____
_____
_____

Reading The Scarlet Letter

Name: _____ Date: _____

The Scarlet Letter, Chapters 9–12 Reading Quiz A

Directions: Below you see several quotations from Chapters 9–12. Please answer each question following the quotations as correctly and thoroughly as possible.

"… they took long walks on the sea-shore, or in the forest; mingling various talk with the plash and murmur of the waves, and the solemn wind-anthem of the tree-tops."

1. What two characters are described here as taking these walks?

   _____
   _____
   _____
   _____
   _____
   _____

"[I found these flora] Even in the grave-yard here at hand … They are new to me. I found them growing on a grave, which bore no tomb-stone, nor other memorial of the dead man, save these ugly weeds, that have taken upon themselves to keep him in remembrance. They grew out of his heart, and typify, if may be, some hideous secret that was buried with him, and which he had done better to confess during his lifetime."

2. Who speaks these sentences?

   _____
   _____
   _____
   _____
   _____
   _____

3. To whom are these sentences spoken?

   _____
   _____
   _____
   _____
   _____
   _____

Name: _____ Date: _____

"Pearl! Little Pearl! . . . Hester! Hester Prynne! Are you there?"

4. Who speaks these sentences?

   _____
   _____
   _____
   _____
   _____
   _____

5. Why is the speaker at this point unsure of Hester and Pearl's presence?

   _____
   _____
   _____
   _____
   _____
   _____

6. In the lodging shared by two of the story's characters, as described in Chapter 9, there hangs a tapestry; what two Biblical characters are woven into that tapestry?

   _____
   _____
   _____
   _____
   _____
   _____

Reading The Scarlet Letter

Name: _____ Date: _____

The Scarlet Letter, Chapters 9–12 Reading Quiz B

Directions: Below you see several quotations from Chapters 9–12. Please answer each question following the quotations as correctly and thoroughly as possible. Good luck!

"... they discussed every topic of ethics and religion, of public affairs, and private character; they talked much, on both sides, of matters that seemed personal to themselves..."

1. What two characters are here described as having these kinds of discussions?

   _____
   _____
   _____
   _____
   _____
   _____

"Come away, or yonder Black Man will catch you! He hath got hold of the minister already."

2. Who speaks these sentences?

   _____
   _____
   _____
   _____
   _____
   _____

3. To whom are these sentences spoken?

   _____
   _____
   _____
   _____
   _____
   _____

Name: _____ Date: _____

"Who is that man [?] . . . I shiver at him! Dost thou know the man? I hate him [!] I tell thee, my soul shivers at him! . . . Who is he? Who is he? Canst thou do nothing for me? I have a nameless horror of the man!"

4. Who speaks these sentences?

   _____
   _____
   _____
   _____
   _____
   _____
   _____

5. Who is "that man" described by these sentences?

   _____
   _____
   _____
   _____
   _____
   _____
   _____

6. Please describe one example of *dramatic* irony from the conclusion of Chapter 12.

   _____
   _____
   _____
   _____
   _____
   _____
   _____

Reading The Scarlet Letter   **83**

Name: _____ Date: _____

The Scarlet Letter, Chapters 13–15 Reading Quiz A

Directions: Below you see several quotations from Chapters 13–15. Please answer each question following the quotations as correctly and thoroughly as possible.

"In all seasons of calamity, indeed, whether general or of individuals, the outcast of society at once found her place. She came, not as a guest, but as a rightful inmate, into the household that was darkened by trouble; as if its gloomy twilight were a medium in which she was entitled to hold intercourse with her fellow-creatures."

1. As Chapter 13 opens, how old is Pearl?

2. According to this portion of the novel, what is Hester's "place" which she has "found"?

3. Interpret based on your answer to #2: Why is Hester "a rightful inmate" of her "place"?

Name: _____   Date: _____

4. What do the townspeople of Boston now say Hester's letter "A" signifies or means, and why does this interpretation make sense based on your answers to #2 and #3?

_____
_____
_____
_____
_____
_____

"... while uttering these words, [he] lifted his hands with a look of horror, as if he beheld some frightful shape, which he could not recognize, usurping the place of his own image in a glass. It was one of those moments—which sometimes occur only at the interval of years—when a man's moral aspect is faithfully revealed to his mind's eye."

5. Who is the "he" described here?

_____
_____
_____
_____
_____
_____

6. To whom is he "uttering . . . words" at this point of the novel?

_____
_____
_____
_____
_____
_____

7. Near the conclusion of Chapter 15, what does Hester do for the very first time since she was condemned to wear the scarlet letter?

_____
_____
_____
_____
_____

Reading The Scarlet Letter

Name: _____ Date: _____

The Scarlet Letter, Chapters 13–15 Reading Quiz B

Directions: Below you see several quotations from Chapters 13–15. Please answer each question following the quotations as correctly and thoroughly as possible.

"In all seasons of calamity, indeed, whether general or of individuals, the outcast of society at once found her place. She came, not as a guest, but as a rightful inmate, into the household that was darkened by trouble; as if its gloomy twilight were a medium in which she was entitled to hold intercourse with her fellow-creatures."

1. As Chapter 13 opens, how old is Pearl?

2. According to this portion of the novel, what is Hester's "place" which she has "found"?

3. Interpret based on your answer to #2: Why is Hester "a rightful inmate" of her "place"?

Name: _____ Date: _____

4. What do the townspeople of Boston now say Hester's letter "A" signifies or means, and why does this interpretation make sense based on your answers to #2 and #3?

_____
_____
_____
_____
_____
_____

"Peace . . . peace! . . . It is not granted me to pardon. I have no such power as thou tellest me of. My old faith, long forgotten, comes back to me, and explains all that we do, and all we suffer. By thy first step awry, thou didst plant the germ of evil; but since that moment, it has all been a dark necessity."

5. Who speaks these sentences?

_____
_____
_____
_____
_____
_____

6. To whom is he or she speaking at this point of the novel?

_____
_____
_____
_____
_____
_____

7. Near the conclusion of Chapter 15, what does Hester do for the very first time since she was condemned to wear the scarlet letter?

_____
_____
_____
_____
_____
_____

Reading The Scarlet Letter

Name: _____ Date: _____

The Scarlet Letter, Chapters 16–20 Reading Quiz A

Directions: Below you see several quotations from Chapters 16–20. Please answer each question following the quotations as correctly and thoroughly as possible.

"Hester! Hester Prynne! . . . Is it thou? Art thou in life?"

1. Who speaks these sentences?

   _____
   _____
   _____
   _____
   _____
   _____
   _____

2. In what physical location/space are these sentences spoken?

   _____
   _____
   _____
   _____
   _____
   _____
   _____

"Thou shalt not go alone!"

3. Who speaks this sentence?

   _____
   _____
   _____
   _____
   _____
   _____
   _____

Name: _____ Date: _____

4. To whom is this sentence spoken?

_____

_____

_____

_____

_____

_____

"The next time, I pray you to allow me only a fair warning, and I shall be proud to bear you company. Without taking overmuch upon myself, my good word will go far towards gaining any strange gentleman a fair reception from yonder potentate you wot of! . . . Ha, ha, ha! . . . Well, well, we must needs talk thus in the daytime! You carry it off like an old hand!"

5. Who speaks these sentences?

_____

_____

_____

_____

_____

_____

6. To whom are these sentences spoken?

_____

_____

_____

_____

_____

_____

Name: _____ Date: _____

The Scarlet Letter, Chapters 16–20 Reading Quiz B

Directions: Below you see several quotations from Chapters 16–20. Please answer each question following the quotations as correctly and thoroughly as possible.

"So strangely did they meet . . . that it was like the first encounter, in the world beyond the grave, of two spirits who had been intimately connected in their former life, but now stood coldly shuddering, in mutual dread, as not yet familiar with their state, nor wonted to the companionship of disembodied beings. Each a ghost, and awe-stricken at the other ghost!"

1. What two persons meet here as "ghosts"?

   _____
   _____
   _____
   _____
   _____
   _____

2. Where (i.e., in what physical space/location) do these two ghost-persons here meet?

   _____
   _____
   _____
   _____
   _____
   _____

"Preach! Write! Act! Do anything, save to lie down and die!"

3. Who speaks these sentences?

   _____
   _____
   _____
   _____
   _____
   _____

Name: _____ Date: _____

4. To whom are these sentences spoken?

_____
_____
_____
_____
_____
_____

"The next time, I pray you to allow me only a fair warning, and I shall be proud to bear you company. Without taking overmuch upon myself, my good word will go far towards gaining any strange gentleman a fair reception from yonder potentate you wot of! . . . Ha, ha, ha! . . . Well, well, we must needs talk thus in the daytime! You carry it off like an old hand!"

5. Who speaks these sentences?

_____
_____
_____
_____
_____
_____

6. To whom are these sentences spoken?

_____
_____
_____
_____
_____
_____

Reading The Scarlet Letter

Name: _____ Date: _____

The Scarlet Letter, Chapters 21–24 Reading Quiz A

Directions: Below you see several quotations from Chapters 21–24. Please answer each question following the quotations as correctly and thoroughly as possible.

"... I must bid the steward make ready one more berth than you bargained for!"

1. What person is speaking here?

   _____
   _____
   _____
   _____
   _____
   _____

2. To what other person does he or she speak?

   _____
   _____
   _____
   _____
   _____
   _____

3. What is the meaning of this quotation (i.e., what is being discussed here)?

   _____
   _____
   _____
   _____
   _____
   _____

Name: _____ Date: _____

"ON A FIELD, SABLE, THE LETTER A, GULES."

4. What is the importance of this quotation (i.e., what is its significance in the novel)?

_____
_____
_____
_____
_____
_____

Name: _____ Date: _____

The Scarlet Letter, Chapters 21–24 Reading Quiz B

Directions: Below you see several quotations from Chapters 21–24. Please answer each question following the quotations as correctly and thoroughly as possible.

"Let me now do the will which he hath made plain before my sight. . . . So let me make haste to take my shame upon me!"

1. What person is speaking here?

   _____
   _____
   _____
   _____
   _____
   _____
   _____

2. To what other person does he or she speak?

   _____
   _____
   _____
   _____
   _____
   _____
   _____

3. What is the narrative importance of this quotation (i.e., at what point of the novel's plot does this quotation arise)?

   _____
   _____
   _____
   _____
   _____
   _____
   _____

Name: _____ Date: _____

"ON A FIELD, SABLE, THE LETTER A, GULES."

4. What is the importance of this quotation (i.e., what is its significance in the novel)?

   _____
   _____
   _____
   _____
   _____
   _____

Reading The Scarlet Letter

Chapter 4

Understanding *The Scarlet Letter*

Surely most teachers who have previously led students through a reading of *The Scarlet Letter* have encountered and had to overcome students' difficulties with the text, be they caused by grammatical complexities, comprehension issues, or simple apathy. Reading through the novel is one thing, but grasping and understanding its artistry and relevance to the modern age, if not outright human timelessness, is on another level altogether. Thus, I have distinguished between activities and assignments highlighting the novel's events and aiming at reading comprehension at an introductory "surface" level, all in the previous chapter, and share approaches to the novel aimed at a deeper understanding of it in this chapter. In addition, although the last chapter was organized chronologically, according to the novel's sequential chapters, this one, in addition to all subsequent chapters, is organized by topic of inquiry.

This chapter is essentially divided into two halves: one half of text, written largely to assist your purposes in aiding students' comprehension of Hawthorne's style, and one of prompts and activities, the purpose of which is assignment to students various tasks to enhance their appreciation for the novel's artistry and relevance to their own lives.

Difficulties With Hawthorne's Grammar

Facing and overcoming the obstacles posed by Nathaniel Hawthorne's large and admittedly somewhat antiquated vocabulary is definitely one issue facing many young readers of *The Scarlet Letter*, but interpreting his similarly challenging grammatical patterns, including both punctuation usage and syntactical architecture, provides a different difficulty altogether. There are several elements to Hawthorne's writing style that, in my experience, commonly trip up student readers, and I have attempted here to describe and analyze them separately.

Archaisms

It surely goes without saying, but Hawthorne wrote beautifully in the English of his era, if not an even earlier one. Modern readers encounter in *The Scarlet Letter* not only a 200-year-old variance from our contemporary prose, but also, and even more confusingly, a conflation of 19th century and mid-17th century Englishes. Why? Hawthorne's own narration is of course written in the language of his day, which differs to some noticeable degrees from students' modern English, but his search for characteristic authenticity also caused Hawthorne to compose his characters' speech in the language of their own setting. Thus, in a linguistic "telephone game" of sorts, today's readers are approximately 200 years removed from their novelist's prose, which is itself an additional 200 years removed, give or take, from his characters' dialogue. The difficulties of keeping up with the story's goings-on is thus compounded.

For example, consider the following excerpt from Chapter XIX: "The Child at the Brook-Side":

> "Thou strange child, why dost thou not come to me?" exclaimed Hester.
> Pearl still pointed with her forefinger; and a frown gathered on her brow; the more impressive from the childish, the almost baby-like aspect of the features that conveyed it. [...]
> "Hasten, Pearl; or I shall be angry with thee!" cried Hester Prynne, who, however inured to such behavior on the elf-child's part at other seasons, was naturally anxious for a more seemly deportment now. "Leap across the brook, naughty child, and run hither! Else I must come to thee!"
> But Pearl, not a whit startled at her mother's threats, any more than mollified by her entreaties, now suddenly burst into a fit of passion, gesticulating violently, and throwing her small figure into the most extravagant contortions. [...]
> "I pray you," answered the minister, "if thou hast any means of pacifying the child, do it forthwith! Save it were the cankered wrath of an old witch, like Mistress Hibbins," added he, attempting to smile, "I know nothing that I would not sooner encounter than this passion in a child." (p. 134)

Dissecting this short passage, we can see clearly the diffusion of language into two separate English epochs, so to speak. Hawthorne's own narration resembles modern English, though it is certainly made difficult by the inclusion of words such as "mollified," "gesticulating," "seemly," and "deportment." High-level diction, such as these examples, is addressed in Chapter 3 of this book, and difficulties arising from such vocabulary is soon overcome with word study.

Considering the spoken dialogue in this passage, however, we see English of another sort. The characters' diction more closely resembles that of Shakespeare than of Hawthorne himself, as seen clearly in Hester's and Dimmesdale's usage of archaic pronouns (e.g., "Thou" and "thee"), antiquated expressions (e.g., "run hither," "I pray you," and "Else I must"), and outdated verbs and their conjugations (e.g., "dost," "Hasten," and "hast"), not to mention anachronistically odd vocabulary in general (e.g., "forthwith").

Students today must therefore comprehend artistically rich language for the sake of following Hawthorne's prose, yes, but also subdivide that language throughout the novel into separate "forms." Whereas the earlier of these forms of English, that spoken by the characters themselves, perhaps sets forth the most antiquated diction, it is actually Hawthorne's narration of events that provides the most challengingly confusing usage of punctuation.

Punctuation

Consider again that selected passage from Chapter XIX. Punctuation used to convey Hester's initial question to Pearl is identical to how we today would use punctuation in writing the same sentence. The next sentence, however, utilizes two semicolons where we today would use commas. Semicolons in modern English grammar are used to join together two independent clauses (i.e., two complete statements capable of standing alone as full sentences). Here, however, Hawthorne interjects a correlative conjunction, "and," after the first semicolon, thereby rendering the clause dependent, and utilizes a second semicolon to introduce a long extraneous description, resembling an appositive, where we once again would today utilize a comma.

These discrepancies might be considerable as minor issues. After all, if students simply read along with the words and pause when directed to do so by punctuation marks of any sort, then they shall follow the plot's progression finely. However, any AP students concerned with punctuation—and don't we want all of them to be?—face the danger of interruptions to their reading, invariably the results of irregularity-caused moments of confusion. At that same point of the selected passage, to wit, Hawthorne uses a semicolon to introduce "the more impressive from," then immediately uses a comma to introduce "the almost baby-like aspect of." Both of these phrases begin with the same article, both of them center upon adjectives, and both of them conclude with prepositions; their constructions are essentially the same, observant students may notice, so why on Earth the difference in punctuation? Sprinkle such irregularities throughout the book, and you may have a classroom full of confused grammarians.

Their confusion is potentially exacerbated further because Hawthorne appears to vary which types of punctuation marks he uses in lieu of commas at various points of the novel. Consider, for example, the story's opening, from "The Custom-House: Introductory to *The Scarlet Letter*" chapter:

> It is a little remarkable, that—though disinclined to talk overmuch of myself and my affairs at the fireside, and to my personal friends—an autobiographical impulse should twice in my life have taken possession of me, in addressing the public. The first time was three or four years since, when I favored the reader—inexcusably, and for no earthly reason, that either the indulgent reader or the intrusive author could imagine—with a description of my way of life in the deep quietude of an Old Manse. And now—because, beyond my deserts, I was happy enough to find a listener or two on the former occasion—I again seize the public by the button, and talk of my three years' experience in a Custom-House. (p. 7)

Every one of the dashes used in these three sentences signals some sort of interjection or extraneous description, but not one of them is grammatically . . . I won't say appropriate, but necessary. It appears that Hawthorne has simply chosen to *replace* a number of commas in this passage, for every one of these dashes might instead take the form of a comma and lose not one bit of meaning or syntactical clarity. In Chapter XIX, particularly in the passage by the brook-side previously analyzed, Hawthorne uses semicolons in place of commas, but here he uses dashes to the same effect. Why? A self-assured student might simply answer, "to keep us on our toes." Truth be told, an answer resorting to such arbitrariness may not be too far off base.

On the other hand, many students might not mind the occasional inclusion of a stray semicolon here and there, for Hawthorne's legacy as a difficult read rests upon, among other things, his "overuse" of commas. Consider another selection from "The Custom-House: Introductory to *The Scarlet Letter*":

> But, as thoughts are frozen and utterance benumbed, unless the speaker stands in some true relation with his audience, it may be pardonable to imagine that a friend, a kind and apprehensive, though not the closest friend, is listening to our talk; and then, a native reserve being thawed by this genial consciousness, we may prate of the circumstances that lie

around us, and even of ourself, but still keep the inmost Me behind its veil. (p. 7)

That's one sentence, including 10 commas and a semicolon. The purpose of it? Simply to describe Hawthorne's ideal reader, we as teachers might say. Simply to use a bunch of commas, our students might say.

Contrary to that perception, like any accomplished engineer in any constructive field, Hawthorne is in fact using punctuation in multitudinous cases throughout the novel so that he can build sentences within sentences, descriptions within descriptions, all to design architecturally beautiful syntax. Students may find it odd to describe sentences with words such as "geometric" or "symmetry," but these words are appropriate in Hawthorne's case. Take, for example, Dimmesdale's statement to Chillingworth in Chapter X: "The Leech and His Patient":

"There can be, if I forebode aright, no power, short of the Divine mercy, to disclose, whether by uttered words, or by type or emblem, the secrets that may be buried with a human heart. The heart, making itself guilty of such secrets, must perforce hold them, until the day when all hidden things shall be revealed. Nor have I so read or interpreted Holy Writ, as to understand that the disclosure of human thoughts and deeds, then to be made, is intended as a part of the retribution. That, surely, were a shallow view of it. No; these revelations, unless I greatly err, are meant merely to promote the intellectual satisfaction of all intelligent beings, who will stand waiting, on that day, to see the dark problem of this life made plain." (p. 88)

The five sentences composing this passage contain their share of commas, yes, but each comma in this case clearly serves Hawthorne's purpose. Just as commas in modern usage surround and therefore indicate the presence of simple appositive phrases (e.g., "Bob, my friend, is tall"), interjections (e.g., "Bob, thank goodness, is tall"), relative and otherwise dependent clauses (e.g., "Bob, who is young, is tall"), and direct addresses (e.g., "Listen, Bob, when I am talking to you"), Hawthorne's commas in this passage similarly highlight offset phrases and clauses. For example, in the first sentence of this passage, an elimination of every phrase and clause encapsulated within commas yields the central comment of the sentence: "There can be [. . .] no power [. . .] to disclose [. . .] the secrets that may be buried with a human heart." Now, *this* sentence makes a bit more straightforward sense! Once the keystone clause of any sentence is in this way apprehended by a student, then he or she need only review what extraneous clauses and phrases were contained by commas in the first place in order to see Hawthorne's purposes. Like a clausal palindrome, the narration of *The Scarlet Letter* is consistently dissectible in this way throughout the tale, and your students' understanding of the architecture will certainly enable them more fully to comprehend Hawthorne's syntactical artistry.

Atmospheric Verbs

Readers of contemporary literature are accustomed to adjectival and adverbial usage, particularly for purposes of description. As youngsters, many students are taught that the simplest and most effective way to add descriptive details to their own writing is to pile on appropriate adjectives and adverbs. Thereby, a 7-year-old's sentence stating that "My sister drove to the beach" becomes the elaborative "My beautiful older sister drove quickly and safely to the hot, crowded, fun beach."

Hawthorne does use a number of adjectives and adverbs thusly, it is true, but students unused to his or his contemporaries' style sometimes miss out on perhaps the most common atmospheric descriptor that he uses: the verb itself. In Chapter II: "The Marketplace," for example, consider the following account of Hester's passage from the jail to the central scaffold:

> It was no great distance, in those days, from the prison-door to the market-place. Measured by the prisoner's experience, however, it might be reckoned a journey of some length; for, haughty as her demeanor was, she perchance underwent an agony from every footstep of those that thronged to see her, as if her heart had been flung into the street for them all to spurn and trample upon. (p. 41)

The only descriptive adjective of note in these sentences is "haughty," and there are no adverbs here. Nevertheless, the atmosphere of central Boston, as well as the clear antagonism between Hester and the assembled crowd, is clear and powerful, created almost entirely through Hawthorne's choices of strongly articulate, descriptive verbs. "Measured" and "reckoned," for example, convey an action of slow calculation and intricacy, as if every step that Hester takes on her way is separable, noticeable, and notable for its importance and difficulty; moreover, "reckoned" connotatively suggests "reckoning," which of course carries with it a religious underpinning, apropos of Puritan Massachusetts. The verb "underwent" communicates a similar connotative meaning, as of undergoing a trial, hardship, or even physical torture. Members of the crowd did not just assemble or gather to watch Hester, but rather "thronged" in a communal desire to "spurn and trample upon" the woman's heart, "flung" without care to the figurative wolves.

Asking students to identify descriptive words may in the case of Nathaniel Hawthorne trip them up a bit, for just this reason: contrary to their potential instincts, a search for adjectives may prove less effective than careful attention to the verbs themselves. Not every passage of text follows this pattern, of course, just as not every semicolon or dash in *The Scarlet Letter* is properly replaceable by a comma. That being said, discussing with your students these common difficulties, patterns, and approaches to comprehension should go a long way in aiding their understanding of the text and its author's artistry beyond a simple focus on vocabulary or plot development.

Lesson Plan: The Importance of Being Allusive

In addition to the linguistic difficulties facing modern readers of *The Scarlet Letter*, the abundance of allusions by Hawthorne to historical, Biblical, and otherwise extraneously important people and events can prove overwhelming to modern readers unversed in them. This lesson plan is intended to help students to identify, research, and understand not only the allusions themselves, but also Hawthorne's probable motivation for including each one in the novel. Thus, your students will engage both in a research and presentation process and in an evaluation of the author's purposes as an artist. This lesson plan is included on pages 108–111.

Self-Reflective Prompts

As a teacher, I believe that any literary work, regardless of its historical and/or aesthetic reputation, no matter how much of a classic it is said to be, in the end aids student readers very little unless it contributes in some meaningful way to their own understandings of themselves and their lives. Details regarding a plot, characters, conflicts, or symbolism are in the final equation less important than the most significant inquiry made by teenagers encountering any book, play, or poem in English class: "What does this have to do with me?" Teachers who help their students to find the answer to that question give to those students what is in my opinion the greatest gift that an English teacher can bestow: an understanding of the *personal* value of a literary education.

To this end, I believe it is always important to allow students time to reflect upon literature not just as historical pieces from bygone eras and places, distinct and detached from the modern teenage world, but also as mirrors to be considered honestly and individually, as reflective works able to demonstrate any adolescent's connection to the larger human family and the quintessential human experience, regardless of how disconnected from them he or she may feel.

The questions that follow offer students just that opportunity to examine themselves and their lives in the mirror of *The Scarlet Letter*. They are not literary analysis questions in an academic sense, but rather entrees to bibliotherapy, a process of self-reflection and catharsis through literature that certainly most English teachers have utilized in our own educations. I personally believe that when students are asked to consider topics such as the ones below, their responses should not be evaluated, perhaps not even collected or read by the teacher at all; privacy and personal safety, after all, engender honesty. You might find it useful for that purpose to ask that your students spread out in their classroom or other quiet place, writing individually and silently upon the chosen topic for 10 minutes or so, after which time they could safely pack their private responses away and move on to the next class activity. On the other hand, you could just as easily assign responses to these prompts for homework. Whatever approach to this bibliotherapy you choose to take, I advise that you create a safe environment for students' self-reflection and metacognition, an academic situation in which they do not feel threatened by imminent grades, the perceptions of their peers, or perhaps even a perusal of their personal statements by you, the teacher. In my view, for gifted teenagers full of extensive emotional overexcitabilities, opportunities to write sincerely and safely are not only valuable, but also quite worth protecting.

- Which of the novel's characters do you feel that you understand best and/or can connect with most easily? Explain why.
- What or whom do you personally feel is most to blame for the heartache of the novel's characters? Whose fault is it all really?
- Do you believe that Hester and Chillingworth ever really loved each other? If so, then what happened? If not, then why might they have wed in the first place?
- Do you blame Roger Chillingworth for his actions throughout the novel? Why, or why not?
- Have you personally ever felt trapped by something from your past from which you could not escape? If so, then what were the circumstances, and how did you ultimately deal with the situation?
- Dimmesdale's pain throughout the tale is of course caused by his omnipresent guilt. Have you ever felt so contritely mournful over something done that it affected your health? If so, then what were the circumstances, and how did you ultimately deal with them?
- Have you ever, like Chillingworth, felt betrayed by someone who is supposed to love you? What were the circumstances, and what was their outcome?

Taxonomical Worksheets

I believe that in general, worksheets as a scholastic tool have a poor reputation among teachers of gifted and talented students; these teachers perhaps see the worksheet as prepackaged busywork for instructors lacking the abilities or desire to design their own assessments or engage their classes interpersonally. Truth be told, I myself have felt similarly about prepackaged "busywork," but as with most stereotypes, this idea that all worksheets are created equally poorly is probably untrue and unfair. In fact, such instruments composed not of tediously repetitive exercises, but rather of cognitive tasks designed to stretch students' intellectual reasoning, scholarly abilities, and creativity can actually be terrific formative devices. I have to this end designed and included five worksheets that reward students' engagement in increasingly demanding creative and otherwise cognitive tasks. I constructed these worksheets based on the concept of taxonomically organized intellectual processes, and they are designed so that the more challenging the task is that a student completes, the more he or she is rewarded in the grade book.

Please note that these worksheets are not based upon any singular taxonomy of cognitive processes, but they resemble all such taxonomies in their hierarchy of intellectual tasks that escalate in difficulty. Students desirous to earn the highest scores on these worksheets are therefore obligated to complete not only the task attached to the desired grade, but also those assignments "below" that goal on the worksheet. Thus, highly motivated students who complete these worksheets in their entireties can earn A grades, interpreting and responding to *The Scarlet Letter* in a diversity of ways and utilizing everything from their comprehension of basic plot events to their ability to formulate and defend judgments on entirely subjective interpretive topics.

Every task required of students who wish to earn a D- calls for a provision of factual details in response to a simple text-based question or prompt; beyond that lowest-level question, though, there certainly are any number of legitimate ways in which students can answer every other question or complete each task on these worksheets. By and large, then, there is almost never a singular "right answer" to any of these items. Therefore, teachers should regard each student's answers and responses individually, evaluating their legitimacy relative to *The Scarlet Letter* itself, not solely to other students' answers and responses.

As students approach the highest-level tasks, pay close attention to directions and questions requiring the consideration of multiple parts (e.g., the fulfillment of an assigned task *plus* the provision of textual support to defend one's product). Students completing only half of the requirements should not be credited for the full completion of that particular task. Additionally, students should complete all of the tasks and answer all of the questions leading up to the one for which they wish to earn the highest grade; one should not earn an A, for example, if he or she has not completed all of the other tasks also. Your highest-achieving students, then, will assuredly engage in a great variety of intellectual activities on their way to earning that grade and resultant understanding of the novel.

The taxonomical worksheets can be found at the end of this chapter, on pages 112–121.

Conclusion

The worksheets that follow, as all of the information already in this chapter, will aid your students in preparing for academic activities found in later chapters, where they will apply their understanding of *The Scarlet Letter* and its intricacies in numerous ways both oral and written.

Chapter Materials

LESSON 2

Lesson Plan:
The Importance of Being Allusive

Purpose/Objective
This activity will aid students' understanding of *The Scarlet Letter* by helping to illumine various historical and Biblical allusions made by Hawthorne throughout the novel. Students will develop their research and presentation skills, as well as their note-taking abilities.

Placement
This lesson can be completed at any time during your students' studies of the novel, but will of course be more impactful the earlier it is assigned. An ideal placement of the lesson might be immediately following students' encounter with the first chapter, for they could then investigate Anne Hutchinson, determine her symbolic import to Hawthorne and his literary purpose (i.e., why he chose to allude to her in this case), and thusly develop a framework for exploring other allusions and utilizing their findings throughout the novel.

Materials Required
For the research component of this lesson, you will require either hard copy resources, such as encyclopedias, history textbooks, or even the Bible itself, or computers enabled with Internet access, allowing students to conduct online research.

Duration
If completed fully in class, this activity should require approximately 2 hours, including all research and presentations. If all research is conducted independently (i.e., for homework), then the necessary time spent in class will, of course, be shortened.

Lesson Plan
1. *Anticipatory Set*: Ask students to brainstorm in their notebooks as many famous quotations from American history as possible. As examples, you might offer such standbys as "We have nothing to fear but fear itself" or "We hold these truths to be self-evident." After allowing them approximately 2–3 minutes to brainstorm and create their lists, have them share their results with partners and then ask for volunteers to share their favorite responses with the class as a whole. As a secondary step, assign them to a different task: They should write in their notebooks a brief letter to the

editor, mock newspaper article, or pretend blog entry on a topic of their choice in which they utilize at least four of the famous quotations that arose from the class or their own brainstorming; in other words, while writing about whatever topic is of interest to them in their small product, allude to these famous moments of American history by utilizing the words themselves. After allowing approximately 8–10 minutes of silent writing, ask your students to share their results with one another and then the entire class in the same way as previously. All told, this anticipatory set will take approximately 20–30 minutes, but will lay solid groundwork for your students' understanding of and work with literary allusions.

2. *Communication of Objective*: After discussing what a literary allusion is—after all, they just concocted a number of them in their brief written products—inform the class that one reason why *The Scarlet Letter* commonly confuses modern readers is that Hawthorne interjected into his novel a number of allusions to historical or Biblical persons, places, or other items, many of which are unfamiliar to even the academic majority. The goal of this lesson, therefore, is not only to investigate some of the most prominent of these allusions, but also to evaluate why Hawthorne might have chosen to incorporate them into his novel at the particular points that he did.

3. *Division of Labor:* You will need students or groups of students who are responsible for investigating and making choices about all of the following historical or Biblical persons, images, or places. In each case, you should provide your researchers with only the name or description given, plus the approximate date or literary source provided. Thus, keeping your provision of primary information to students so small, you will ensure via the approximate date or source given that they at least identify the correct person, phrase, or location, rather than get sidetracked by unrelated people of the same name, while at the same time not making students' research process overly easy. Thus, please divide your class into 12 such groups:
    1. Eden (Biblical book of Genesis)
    2. Cain (Biblical book of Genesis)
    3. Enoch (Biblical book of Genesis)
    4. Bathsheba (Biblical book of II Samuel)
    5. a Pearl of Great Price (Biblical Gospel of Matthew)
    6. Martin Luther (circa 1515)
    7. Thomas Overbury (circa 1615)
    8. Anne Hutchinson (circa 1630)
    9. Richard Bellingham (circa 1640)
    10. John Winthrop (circa 1640)
    11. Ann Hibbins (circa 1650)
    12. Elizabeth Pain / Payne (circa 1690)

LESSON 2

4. *Research and Artifact Gathering:* If you wish to accomplish this portion of the lesson in class, then allow your students approximately 45 minutes to one hour to research their respective persons, locations, or items. Assign the students the responsibility not only to discover background details about their particular area of research, but to prepare a presentation to the class in terms of a story; their presentation to classmates should therefore frame their particular subject's importance within some sort of narrative, including a beginning, a middle, and an end; the narrative should essentially detail how, why, and under what conditions this individual topic became important according to its particular source for research. If you wish to require some sort of visual element to the presentation, then this narrative can of course be graphically represented alongside key details of the given subject's historical or Biblical importance. This portion of the lesson may also be accomplished for homework.

5. *Presentations*: The next portion of this activity requires that students present their research to one another. Students should take down notes based on each other's findings so that they essentially compile a research or study guide to aid their understandings of the various allusions that arise throughout the novel. In my own classes, I believe that beginning with Anne Hutchinson is both an appropriate and a helpful way to start the cycle of students' presentations, for despite Hutchinson's relative lateness in history, her allusion is the first to arise in the main plot of the novel. Therefore, deciphering her literary import or effect at the moment of Hawthorne's allusion to her can serve the rest of the class as a model approach to the next step of the lesson.

6. *Evaluation of Purpose*: Once students have communicated to one another the backgrounds and significances of all of the selected allusions, their respective meanings within the context of *The Scarlet Letter* should be considered. In other words, it is surely not helpful enough simply to know who Anne Hutchinson was and why she is notable; rather, it is more useful to consider all of that information relative to when Hawthorne's allusion to her arises in the novel, judging what he uses that allusion to accomplish. Students' grades, in this respect, might be compiled twofold: on the one hand, they can be rewarded for adequate research and presentation of their findings, but in another way, they might earn marks for identifying the points of the allusions' appearances, evaluating Hawthorne's literary purposes in making the allusions, and utilizing textual details from those particular moments of *The Scarlet Letter* to support their evaluations. Again, beginning with the early allusion to Anne Hutchinson provides a model for the rest of the class in this respect, for it can clearly be seen that Hawthorne alludes to the woman in Chapter I in order to compare her

to Hester Prynne, and thus to associate immediately for the reader the novel's protagonist with "the sainted Ann Hutchinson" of history (p. 37).

Closure

You may choose to have students synthesize several of these allusions and their respective evaluations of purpose into a longer essay considering how, in general, literary allusions aid Hawthorne's communication of his tale and message; otherwise, you could effectively approach the same large-scale analysis of allusive usage in the novel via a graded seminar discussion. Resources for assigning and assessing various kinds of essays can be found in Chapter 6: Writing About *The Scarlet Letter*, found on pages 143–181, and similar directions and resources for holding graded seminar discussions can be found in Chapter 5: Talking About *The Scarlet Letter*, found on pages 123–141.

Name: _____ Date: _____

Taxonomical Worksheet for "The Custom-House: Introductory to *The Scarlet Letter*"

Directions: Please use only the spaces provided to the right of each task/question.

To get an **A** on this assignment, you must accomplish this task, plus all of the ones below	The particular views that Hawthorne expresses about individual people and circumstances in "The Custom-House: Introductory to *The Scarlet Letter*" can be extrapolated and interpreted to represent his similar views on related, albeit more general, topics. Consider specifically his expressed thoughts and feelings about the deceased, physical places and things from the past, people and positions of authority, and his chosen literary career. Please evaluate, based on evidence from the chapter, Hawthorne's consideration of these four elements, considering particularly about which of them he feels most and least strongly.	
To get a **B+** on this assignment, you must complete this task, plus all of the ones below	In this introductory chapter, Hawthorne of course describes his political position and occupation prior to his composition of *The Scarlet Letter* itself. Among many other elements considered in "The Custom-House: Introductory to *The Scarlet Letter*," Hawthorne portrays various of his colleagues at that time, including particularly the Inspector, the General, and someone identified as a man of business, all of whom are well characterized herein. Please script an imaginary dialogue among these three persons, based on personality traits and personal interests as provided by Hawthorne. What might these three discuss, and how might they do so?	

Name: _____ Date: _____

To get a **B-** on this assignment, you must complete this task, plus all of the ones below	In your estimation, why did Hawthorne choose to invent a backstory about discovering the scarlet letter itself and a related manuscript? Please consider from the author's point of view what this addition to *The Scarlet Letter* might provide, and justify your answer.	
To get a **C** on this assignment, you must accomplish this task, plus the ones below	Hawthorne in "The Custom-House: Introductory to *The Scarlet Letter*" expresses his view of his Massachusetts ancestors, plus surmises how they might feel about him and his life. Please consider another historical or popular figure who might have an attitude similar to Hawthorne's. In your estimation, how and why are the two persons similar in this respect? Justify your answer(s).	
To get a **D+** on this assignment, you must complete this task, plus the one below	What is Hawthorne's expressed attitude toward his official position and his colleagues at Salem's Custom House, and apparently why? Please answer these questions, utilizing evidence from the introductory chapter.	
To get a **D-** on this assignment, you must accomplish this task	"The Custom-House: Introductory to *The Scarlet Letter*" describes what series of chronological events in Hawthorne's life? Please answer this question, citing particular evidence from the introductory chapter.	

Understanding The Scarlet Letter

Name: _____ Date: _____

Taxonomical Worksheet for Chapters I–VI of *The Scarlet Letter*

Directions: Please use only the spaces provided to the right of each task/question.

To get an **A** on this assignment, you must accomplish this task, plus all of the ones below	After her sentencing upon Boston's central scaffold, Hester chooses within this series of early chapters how she should proceed to live as a member of her Puritan society. Please determine, based on Hawthorne's portrayal of her and her fellow citizens, as well as of Puritanism wholly, whether Hester Prynne's choices are wise, imprudent, risky, or otherwise. Consider matters of both geography and economy, and justify your judgment in the space to the right, utilizing clear logic and supportive details from the novel.	
To get a **B+** on this assignment, you must complete this task, plus all of the ones below	*The Scarlet Letter*, of course, describes a society of early Puritan settlement that is at once both quite removed from our modern culture and very much our ideological and cultural forebear. Consider Hester Prynne's crime, as identified in Chapters I–VI, then place it on two original hierarchies of sins: one suitable for Puritan beliefs and one more acceptable or accustomed to the modern world. How would her sin's position on these hierarchies be similar to or different than one another? Please consider and describe your choices, justifying both your two spectrum's included elements and positional choices with sound logic.	

Name: _____ Date: _____

To get a **B-** on this assignment, you must complete this task, plus all of the ones below	In Chapter I of his novel, Hawthorne identifies two building projects that he highlights as among the first that must be settled upon by any newly founded society. What are these two structures, and what does Hawthorne's choice of them in this regard demonstrate about the people of this book, "amongst whom religion and law were almost identical" (p. 37)? Please analyze this relationship and consider its relevancy in particular to early Massachusetts Puritans.	
To get a **C** on this assignment, you must accomplish this task, plus the ones below	In this series of chapters, Roger Chillingworth expresses his desire to get even for his being wronged and his rights being transgressed. Considering various aspects of characterization, as well as his own dialogue, describe some particular ways in which Chillingworth might be able to concoct retribution, should he prove able to identify the wrongdoer.	
To get a **D+** on this assignment, you must complete this task, plus the one below	Please describe the clothing, personality, and overall characterization of Pearl, Hester Prynne's daughter. Be sure to justify your insights with evidence from the text.	
To get a **D-** on this assignment, you must accomplish this task	What is the relationship in Chapters 1–6, and what was it in previous years, between Hester Prynne and the mysterious stranger whom we come to know as Chillingworth?	

Understanding The Scarlet Letter

Name: _____ Date: _____

Taxonomical Worksheet for Chapters VII–XII of *The Scarlet Letter*

Directions: Please use only the spaces provided to the right of each task/question.

To get an **A** on this assignment, you must accomplish this task, plus all of the ones below	In the final chapter of this series, Chillingworth, Dimmesdale, Pearl, and Hester all meet at Boston's central scaffold. As the scaffold is indicated in the novel's earliest chapters as a place of shame and punishment, this confluence of characters is here fitting. Among the three major adult characters—Chillingworth, Dimmesdale, and Hester Prynne—none is innocent; all are sinful to some degree. Please rank each of these three characters based on their relative levels of culpability, innocence, or punition, per your own criteria. Please explain not only their placement in your hierarchy, but also your reasons for ranking them as you do.	
To get a **B+** on this assignment, you must complete this task, plus all of the ones below	Imagine that throughout the events described in Chapters VII–XII, both Roger Chillingworth and Arthur Dimmesdale pen their innermost thoughts in daily journals or diaries. Please choose one of these two men and write at least three excerpts from his hypothetical journal entries, not only referring to chronologically aligned events from this group of chapters, but also demonstrating your understanding of the character's personality and motivation.	

Name: _____ Date: _____

To get a **B-** on this assignment, you must complete this task, plus all of the ones below	Among the novel's four major characters, the one exhibiting the least amount of self-control is surely Pearl, which is wholly understandable given her young age. Please analyze Pearl's character. What kind of a child is she, why does she act in the ways that she does, and what in truth is the source of her personality? Support your analysis with evidence from the novel.	
To get a **C** on this assignment, you must accomplish this task, plus the ones below	Several symbolic motifs have begun to accrue metaphorical meaning by this point of the novel, including Boston's scaffold, rosebushes and roses, Hester's scarlet A, and even Pearl herself. Consider these four elements, as well as others of which you can think, and propose their metaphorical imports; what might they each symbolize?	
To get a **D+** on this assignment, you must complete this task, plus the one below	What exactly happens to the four main characters on Boston's central scaffold in Chapter XII? How might these happenings be important to the forward movement of the plot, and how are they symbolic or otherwise portentous of the future?	
To get a **D-** on this assignment, you must accomplish this task	Who is Mistress Hibbins, and what is her importance both in the town of Boston and to the story largely? Please support your answer with reference to particular pages of text.	

Understanding The Scarlet Letter

Name: _____ Date: _____

Taxonomical Worksheet for Chapters XIII–XVIII of *The Scarlet Letter*

Directions: Please use only the spaces provided to the right of each task/question.

To get an **A** on this assignment, you must accomplish this task, plus all of the ones below	The plan of action agreed upon in the forest by both Hester Prynne and Arthur Dimmesdale signals a clear turning point in the narrative. It is certain that the plot following this agreement will proceed in a new direction, but what about the two persons themselves, particularly their moral characters? Please consider the decision made in the forest and evaluate whether it and its consequences make Hester Prynne, in your estimation, an ethically better person, or a worse and more sinful one? Please justify your answer with both logic and evidence from the text.	
To get a **B+** on this assignment, you must complete this task, plus all of the ones below	Throughout the novel, Hawthorne's unique narrative technique allows us as readers to read more about Pearl than hear from Pearl. Like many Puritan children, she is in *The Scarlet Letter* seen by the audience more so than heard. Imagine, however, her thoughts. What must Pearl truly be thinking? Compose what you imagine to be Pearl's interior monologue, communicating her ideas, beliefs, and opinions on the events of the novel wholly, but particularly the events of this group of six chapters.	

Name: _____ Date: _____

To get a **B-** on this assignment, you must complete this task, plus all of the ones below	Among the symbolic motifs and metaphorical objects or devices used throughout *The Scarlet Letter*, natural imagery and elements are among the most common. Consider such elements of the natural world, including water, light, and various forms of plant life. In what ways does Hawthorne imbue them with symbolic meaning? Justify your answer with support from this series of chapters.	
To get a **C** on this assignment, you must accomplish this task, plus the ones below	Chillingworth and Dimmesdale are clearly juxtaposed in these six chapters. How readers are meant to consider or value the two mens' differences, however, is less clear. Please interpret how Hawthorne himself apparently wished us to view or judge the two men. Be sure to support your answer with references to particularly telling words and phrases from these chapters.	
To get a **D+** on this assignment, you must complete this task, plus the one below	This group of chapters contains the first instance of Hester ever being untruthful about the meaning and origin of her scarlet A. Where does this lie occur, and why does she tell it?	
To get a **D-** on this assignment, you must accomplish this task	What large decision regarding the future is made jointly in this series of chapters by both Hester and Dimmesdale? Please support your answer with reference to particular pages of text.	

Understanding The Scarlet Letter

Name: _____ Date: _____

Taxonomical Worksheet for Chapters XIX–XXIV of *The Scarlet Letter*

Directions: Please use only the spaces provided to the right of each task/question.

To get an **A** on this assignment, you must accomplish this task, plus all of the ones below	One important criterion to be met by any classic work of literature regards its thematic interpretability. The simpler the book, the less meaningful it may be to a variety of insightful readers, so the more open to interpretation a story is, the more potentiality it has of engendering meaning for a vast and diverse readership. Consider some common analytical methodologies applied to *The Scarlet Letter*, particularly analyses of it as a feminist work, a morally didactic tale, and a historically rich period piece. Please rank these three interpretive approaches in terms of how useful they prove in taking meaning from the tale. Which of these three is the most legitimate or impactful analytical approach, and which is the least?	
To get a **B+** on this assignment, you must complete this task, plus all of the ones below	The climax of *The Scarlet Letter* centers upon Dimmesdale's Election Day Sermon. It is a notably powerful speech delivered on a very important day and culminating in a climactically important outcome. Importantly, while Hawthorne describes for us vividly the tone of this sermon, he communicates not one word of its textual content. Based on tonal descriptions and atmospheric directions from the novel, however, please compose what you imagine Dimmesdale's Election Day Sermon to be. What might Arthur Dimmesdale actually have said?	

Name: _____ Date: _____

To get a **B-** on this assignment, you must complete this task, plus all of the ones below	What are we to make of Pearl's interactions with her father, Arthur Dimmesdale? Near the novel's conclusion, Hawthorne juxtaposes two different interactions between the girl and the minister: one in Chapter XIX, and the other in Chapter XXIII. Please analyze the differences between these two interactions, paying particular attention to their characteristic and symbolic significances.	
To get a **C** on this assignment, you must accomplish this task, plus the ones below	The novel's final image, gazing upon which Hawthorne chooses to fade to black, so to speak, is a tombstone. Notably, while many—if not most—tombstones contain inscribed epitaphs, this one does not. If Pearl were to compose an epitaph for this particular tombstone, then what might it say? Please consider Pearl's point of view and dynamic maturation.	
To get a **D+** on this assignment, you must complete this task, plus the one below	What happens at the Election Day Sermon? Hawthorne himself leaves the answer to that question somewhat ambiguous. From the various perspectives mentioned in the last few chapters, please describe what seems to occur on Election Day, noting distinct characters' different perceptions of the same event.	
To get a **D-** on this assignment, you must accomplish this task	Chapter XXIV of *The Scarlet Letter* is effectively the tale's epilogue, explaining what happens to all of the major characters following the climax of the story. According to this chapter, what happens to each one?	

Understanding The Scarlet Letter

Chapter 5

Talking About *The Scarlet Letter*

As an undergraduate, my experience in English classes was almost entirely discussion-based. Regardless of the contents of a given course—Shakespeare, creative writing, Joyce and Kafka, composition, and so forth—it pedagogically consisted of a large table, a professor seated at its head, around which circled conversations among students. Many former English majors share such recollections, surely, and it is because of such experiences that many of us have decided to become classroom teachers. After all, our literary discipline is an interactive one, if not outright social. Professional organizations in our field recognize as much, which is why the National Board for Professional Teaching Standards requires of aspiring National Board Certified Teachers of English Language Arts twice as many reflective portfolio entries regarding teachers' guidance of students' verbal interactions as regarding their instruction of reading and writing. The National Council of Teachers of English also incorporates dialoguing about literature in its 12 core standards, as does the College Board in its guidelines for AP Literature and Composition teachers. I can thus conclude here, as I have previously, that some of the biggest authorities in English education today view the discussion of literature, incorporating collaborative interplays among students and teachers, as just as important to students' educations as the necessary, all-be-they-solitary, processes of reading and writing about that literature. This proposition is somewhat paradoxical, I know, but what good is an understanding of something if not put to practical (in this case, communal) use?

We teachers fortunate enough to have been involved and engaged, in college or otherwise, in an illuminatingly insightful seminar discussion of literature almost certainly agree. Thinking deeply about literature and the creative process and listening actively and openly to peers' perspectives helps readers to shape opinions and to sharpen interpretive calculi regarding everything from themes to technique and from characters to symbolism. In my opinion, discussions about the literature that we teach form the true core of our professional discipline.

Focusing on two different types of classroom interactions, this chapter investigates several different ways to assign and assess your students' dialogue, including a number of prompts with which to engender conversation. For both cooperative seminar-style discussions and competitive debates, I suggest procedures to establish and follow, questions and prompts to consider, and rubrics and other materials by which to assess students' interactions with one another.

Socratic Seminar

To many classroom teachers, the phrase "Socratic seminar" and the Greek word *paideia* are effectively synonymous. Various scholars and educational leaders distinguish between the two terms and practices, but they are in truth very similar. In both types of exercises, a teacher's instructional role hardly resembles the lecturing "sage on the stage," but instead requires him or her to be either a fellow participant with students or a simple observer and evaluator of their dialogue. When such teachers ask questions in these discussion-based forums, the point is not for students to find the "right" answer, but rather to interact, to bounce theoretical and analytical ideas off one another, to search collaboratively for the meaning of a text—even if that meaning is utterly different for each distinct person in the discussion—and to develop their communicative and analytical skills. When a question is as difficult and open-ended as "Why should we read *The Scarlet Letter* in school, and why does it remain valuable in the modern world?" then a singular "right" answer may well be impossible to find; instead, these seminar discussions allow students to search for and personalize their own "best" answers, which in the end may prove to be more individually lasting and important.

Classroom teachers wishing to utilize seminar discussions pedagogically with their students often face some important and practical classroom issues: How do I make certain that the students will contribute? How do I prevent their reliance upon quick and simple answers? How do I help or account for the shy kids who won't speak up? How are these discussions graded?

A logical and clearly articulated mechanism for evaluating students' participatory dialogue is necessary, and it proves especially beneficial to students who are exposed to it and its criteria before actual graded conversation occurs. Table 4 is a reproducible sheet of grading criteria that I utilize in my own classroom in order to assess seminar discussions.

TABLE 4
Rules and Guidelines for Socratic Seminar

Here are some general rules of thumb:
- The less the teacher has to talk, the better.
- A GOOD seminar looks like 20 people having a fun discussion on a literary topic, as if trying to solve one of the book's "puzzles" together.
- A BAD seminar resembles the Teacher-as-Dentist idea... asking questions should not be like pulling teeth!

Here's How Each Answer Will Be Graded		
Potential Score	Where Your Response Comes From	What Your Response Might Contain
√ ++ (3 pts.)	You reply to other people's responses to the original question, either supporting an argument in agreement or refuting one in polite disagreement.	Your response ties together... - aspects of the discussion to this point, - passages from the text itself, and/or - relevant connections to extraneous studies or observations.
√ + (2 pts.)	You reply to other people's responses to the original question, either supporting an argument in agreement or refuting one in polite disagreement.	Your response is supported either by... - a passage or two from the text itself, or - relevant connections to outside studies or observations.
√ (1 pt.)	Your response is either your individual answer to the initially asked question or a response to another person's answer to the question.	Your response *may* also be supported either by... - textual passages or - relevant connections to outside resources.
√ - (minus 1 pt.)	Your response is solely your individual answer to the initially asked question.	Regardless of the content of your response, it is a repetition of something already said in the discussion.
√ -- (minus 2 pts.)	It is hard to tell, actually...	Your response contains nothing of value; you are talking just to hear yourself.

Modeling appropriate answers of various kinds is also important for successful seminar discussions to occur among students. When I first distribute in my own classroom these grading criteria, I describe to my students what highly successful and less successful seminar discussions "look like," elaborating upon the guidelines bulleted at the top of the page. I then give the class a few moments to peruse the grading criteria, after which I ask them to utilize the sheet in assessing three sample responses to a modeled question: one response is mediocre (1 point), one is outstanding (3 points), and one is silly or immaterial (minus 2 points). This introductory exercise wholly takes approximately 5 minutes prior to our first seminar discussion, but spending that time to clarify my expectations and grading protocol ensures that all students in my class begin the activity with as little anxiety as possible, at least regarding the attached grades; as students begin to talk, I also usually inform the entire class of how I grade the first three or four comments made, further modeling how students' points earned for comments correlate with my printed grading criteria.

My evaluative process is actually very simple. I firstly ask my students to rearrange their desks and chairs into a circle, sitting among them myself with a class roster, which I use to tally checks/points as the discussion proceeds, inserting my own commentary in order to steer the dialogue when appropriate or necessary. Figure 1 is a sample checklist from one of my former AP classes' seminar discussions.

I never like to predetermine the overall point value of a seminar discussion; instead, I involve myself in the dialogue and ultimately conclude its maximum value based on its total quality, as demonstrated by the number of comments made and their relative insights. The seminar discussion exhibited by the checklist in Figure 1 lasted approximately 70 minutes, and I determined based on the quality of students' responses that it should be worth 8 total points. Like any skill necessary for teaching, determining the quantifiable value of any discussion such as this one is potentially difficult at first, but made easier with practice.

The checklist in Figure 1 also reveals several pragmatic issues that require considerable attention. As this log records, during this given seminar, 11 of the 28 students in the class did not contribute to the discussion at all, and only 6 participants earned their full score of 8 points. As all schoolteachers realize, in an activity such as this one there inevitably are going to be students who do not speak up, for any variety of reasons—nervousness, being unprepared, thoughts being elsewhere, etc. I tell my own students prior to their first such discussion with me that I recognize and accept this inevitable fact. "If you know right away that you are simply the type of person who is more likely to sit and listen during this discussion than to speak up and participate," I tell them, "then what I advise is that you take notes on the conversation as it occurs." Elaborating further, I explain to the class that I will allow students who do not contribute commentary to go home that evening and

Kris	Erik
Melissa – ✓, ✓+	Kelsey #3 – ✓, ✓+
Justin	Charlie – ✓+, ✓++, ✓, ✓, ✓
Kelsey #1 – ✓+, ✓+	Garrett
Juliet	Brittany
Corinne – ✓+, ✓++, ✓, ✓+, ✓+	Lily
Johannes	Ashlee – ✓++, ✓, ✓+, ✓++
Pete – ✓, ✓, ✓+	Kyle – ✓, ✓+, ✓++
Kelsey #2 – ✓++, ✓	Ada – ✓+, ✓+, ✓, ✓, ✓+, ✓+
Virginia – ✓+, ✓++, ✓+, ✓+	Amanda
Darian	Hannah – ✓, ✓+, ✓++, ✓
Val	Graham – ✓, ✓, ✓+
Cathryn – ✓	Leah – ✓+, ✓++, ✓
Andrew – ✓+, ✓+, ✓+, ✓+	Jack – ✓+, ✓

Figure 1. Sample assessment checklist from an AP class's Socratic seminar discussion.

write out what they would have said had they participated more in the discussion; the next day, I collect and grade their written responses using the same criteria. A good number of students take advantage of this concession following every graded discussion, especially because I also allow supplemental written commentary from participants who contributed dialogically to some degree, but not enough to garner a perfect score. This policy does lead to additional homework for reserved and otherwise nonparticipatory students, but it also eliminates the inequity that would otherwise arise among extroverted and introverted pupils' scores.

On a related note, it is perhaps also inevitable in classes composed largely of talented and gifted students that certain highly engaged pupils will lead discussions and contribute tremendously more than other classmates will. After all, some people are just more outgoing and loquaciously adventuresome than others. I myself only see a problem with this dialogic inequity when outspoken students dominate seminar discussions to such a degree that other students are actually prevented from contributing, and are therefore prevented from gaining their reasonable share of points. In an attempt to circumvent this foreseeable effect of human nature, I tell my own students—again, before we hold our initial seminar dialogue—that I actually make a point to deduct points from the scores of students who overtly dominate the discussion to a degree detrimental to their classmates. In the cases of particular groups of students that include several highly dominant speakers, I have in the past actually taken to using soccer referees' yellow and red cards to signal to the pupils their statuses in this regard; the showing of a yellow card communicates to students that they are probably nearing their full score of points, and can thus relax, but a red card soon thereafter indicates that they are in fact speaking too often, so much so that if they do not let peers get more words in edgewise, then I shall start to take points away from their total scores. This mechanism provides students with a simple, clear criterion by which to gauge their own participation in any seminar.

In my experience, there are in effect two different types of questions considered in any such classroom seminar discussion: (a) questions considering specifically locatable parts of the text, such as a given chapter or critical moment that isolates important elements such as symbolism, diction, and style; and (b) questions regarding thematically deeper "big picture" issues. The logistics of initiating and assessing students' dialogue really do not vary according to either type of question, but the *contents* of the two types of discussions absolutely do. To the former, tightly focused discussions centering upon particular areas of text utilize numerous supportive quotations and rely upon students' close reading and carefully attentive analysis in order to reach conclusions; to the latter, however, more broadly philosophical and/or thematic discussions refer less frequently to particular moments of dialogue and instead consider works of literature as wholes, examining broader issues that an author imparts over the course of a given story. Presented here are several questions of each type, to all of which, again, there are no particular "right" answers. As I commonly tell my own students prior to engaging in seminars, literary study is not math, and two plus two need not necessarily equal four here.

Textually Based Questions

- What was Hawthorne's apparent goal in writing "The Custom-House: Introductory to *The Scarlet Letter*" and including it as the introductory chapter to this somewhat unrelated story of Puritan Boston?

- Hester decides early in the novel to live apart from her Puritan peers, yet she serves them in various ways throughout the novel. Is her motivation for living apart pride, humility, or something else?

- Chapter VIII introduces Mistress Hibbins, whose presence arises at several points of the novel. What is her importance to *The Scarlet Letter*, as both a character and a symbol?

- Chapter XII, "The Minister's Vigil," is among the most significant in the novel. What is its importance in terms of the plot, the characters, and the overarching themes of *The Scarlet Letter*?

- In Chapter XV, why does Hester choose not to inform Pearl of the scarlet letter's meaning? What conditions are present at this point of the story, preventing Hester's truthfulness, that have not otherwise been so?

- Hawthorne concludes the entire novel with an image of Hester and Dimmesdale's tombstone. What is its significance, as both a physical object and the sole concluding image of the story?

Philosophical and Thematic Questions

- In "The Custom-House," Hawthorne remarks upon the work and necessities of romance writers. In what ways is *The Scarlet Letter* a romantic work of literature?

- How does the symbolism of Hester's scarlet A itself change throughout the course of the novel, and how does that evolution of meaning parallel or otherwise compare to the development of the novel's major characters?

- Puritan society in *The Scarlet Letter* extends outward from its center, which Hawthorne describes in Chapter I as a prison and a cemetery, into uncivilized forest. What layers or "rings" of civilization and wilderness are portrayed in the novel, and what are their significances both geographical and symbolical?

- In what ways does Hawthorne utilize various shadings of light and the presence or absence of colors for symbolic purposes throughout this book?

- In "The Custom-House," Hawthorne describes his own discovery of the scarlet A in order to legitimize the accompanying story as historical. Its various fantastical components and clearly symbolic overtone, however, render the novel as a whole somewhat unrealistic. In your opinion, how did Hawthorne actually intend or hope that his readership would respond to the story of Hester Prynne?

Debate

Socratic seminar discussions are cooperative, enlisting classrooms of students to investigate and solve literary puzzles as a group, but debates between groups of students pitted against each other, on opposite sides of a subjective issue, are competitive. There are various ways to structure debates among students, as there are questions to deliberate, but I am here offering two arrangements for administering classroom debates, both modified from procedures common among competitive debaters across the United States. Some of your students may thusly be familiar with these procedures for interteam debates.

As a simple litmus test, any question to be debated by students in either of the ways here described should be answerable with "yes" or "no." Ultimate victory in a debate round arises not just from students' simple responses to a question itself, of course, but rather from the rhetorical artistry that they utilize to substantiate their answers. Every debate is conducted between two teams of students, the first of which affirms the question (i.e., answers "yes") and the second of which denies it (i.e., answers "no"); according to the tradition of interscholastic debate, I shall here refer to these two student groups as the Affirmative and Negative teams, respectively. In a traditional debate round of this type, each team is composed of two distinct participants, the first and the second speakers, although this number might be expanded to four if necessary in your particular classroom situation.

All four speakers—the 1st and 2nd Affirmative speakers, and the 1st and 2nd Negative speakers—are required to present either one or two speeches each during the debate. If every speaker delivers two speeches, then they are identified as initial Constructive speeches, the purpose of which is to propose and build an argument for one's particular side of the question, and secondary Rebuttal speeches, the purpose of which is to defend one's own argument/case from opposing argumentation (i.e., to rebut the other team's reasoning). A team's first Constructive speeches should be prepared in advance of the debate round, such as homework prior to the classroom debate, and therefore utilize a good amount of textual support for their particular arguments. On the other hand, later rebuttal speeches, and to some extent 2nd Constructive speeches, should be prepared impromptu, as their contents effectively respond to the opposing side's ideas and proposals, about which a debater would not know beforehand. Table 5 is an outline of the

TABLE 5
Debate Round Utilizing Each Speaker Twice

Order of Speeches, Two Per Debater

Name of Speech	Time	Purpose of Speech	Preparation
1st Affirmative Constructive	5 min.	To present the affirmative team's initial case affirming (answering "yes" to) the question.	This speech should be prepared before the debate and include a variety of quotations from the text.
1st Negative Constructive	5 min.	To present the negative team's initial statement denying (answering "no" to) the question.	This speech should be prepared before the debate and include a variety of quotations from the text.
2nd Affirmative Constructive	5 min.	To build further the affirmative team's affirmation of the question, plus to respond to aspects of the negative team's first constructive speech.	Portions of this speech may be prepared before the debate, but parts of it will be impromptu responses to the opposing team's arguments.
2nd Negative Constructive	5 min.	To build further the negative team's denial of the question, plus to respond to aspects of the affirmative team's constructive arguments.	Portions of this speech may be prepared before the debate, but parts of it will be impromptu responses to the opposing team's arguments.
1st Affirmative Rebuttal	2 min.	To rebut any arguments against the affirmative team's case made by the negative team.	This speech will be prepared impromptu.
1st Negative Rebuttal	2 min.	To rebut any arguments against the negative team's case made by the affirmative team.	This speech will be prepared impromptu.
2nd Affirmative Rebuttal	2 min.	To reinforce the affirmative team's case affirming the question, plus to contribute any final remarks upon the negative team's opposing case.	This speech will be prepared impromptu.
2nd Negative Rebuttal	2 min.	To reinforce the negative team's case denying the question, plus to contribute any final remarks upon the affirmative team's opposing case.	This speech will be prepared impromptu.

times allowed for each of the eight speeches, as well as the necessary contents and rhetorical approach of each one.

You may wish to assign questions for homework to your students in advance of the debate, allowing your pupils to prepare their argumentation and support ahead of time, or you may wish to reveal the match-ups at the time of a round, thereby allowing all participants a truncated amount of time to outline an argument and rhetorical approach, find appropriately supportive details from the text, compose a persuasive speech, and anticipate their opponents' contradictory case. Please recognize that while the latter, spur-of-the-moment approach does add

TABLE 6
Debate Round Utilizing Each Speaker Only Once

Order of Speeches, One Per Debater

Name of Speech	Time	Purpose of Speech	Preparation
1st Affirmative	6 min.	To present the affirmative team's initial case affirming (answering "yes" to) the question.	This speech should be prepared before the debate and include a variety of quotations from the text.
1st Negative	6 min.	To present the negative team's initial statement denying (answering "no" to) the question.	This speech should be prepared before the debate and include a variety of quotations from the text.
2nd Affirmative	6 min.	To rebut the negative team's case denying the question, plus to reinforce the affirmative team's case affirming the question.	This speech should be prepared impromptu.
2nd Negative	6 min.	To rebut the affirmative team's case affirming the question, plus to reinforce the negative team's case denying the question.	This speech should be prepared impromptu.

excitement to any debate round, it is practically feasible only with students who know the novel very well and can hastily mine it for effective supportive details.

An alternate arrangement for a classroom debate round allows each student to speak once instead of twice, though for a slightly longer amount of time. The outcome of this second form of debate depends upon the effective delivery of the 2nd Affirmative and Negative speeches, so it is necessary for the second speakers on both teams to be quick-thinking, persuasively polished speakers. Table 6 is an outline of this alternate format for debates.

Regardless of whether you choose for your classroom the arrangement outlined by Table 5 or by Table 6, note that every team engaged in a debate round of any kind should be allowed 4–5 minutes of cooperative preparatory time to use as necessary. During this time, which certainly can be subdivided into smaller chunks useable at various points of a debate round, the teammates might search the novel for evidence supporting their argument, prepare an imminent speech, or discuss strategy. Although the rest of the class might have to sit patiently and wait during this preparatory time, your allowance of it to the debaters will greatly improve the

overall quality of the debate itself. Even for teachers, after all, a moment or two to gather one's thoughts can be worth its weight in gold.

Rather than participating directly in a debate round, judging the argumentation of others can prove to be a very enjoyable and educationally worthwhile role. A limited number of student debaters can participate in each round, of course, so I advise you to allow the remainder of your class to take on the role of judges. Included in Table 7 is a ballot for your students to utilize in this capacity; if many students are filling out individual ballots for themselves, which is probable in most classrooms, then their overall average can of course be used to determine the winning side.

All student judges should utilize the entire ballot in determining a winning side and providing feedback to their peers. That being said, teachers of the gifted may recognize that, human nature being what it is, students' intellectual and academic competitiveness can potentially devolve into inappropriate behavior or commentary. If you choose to include sportsmanship as a quantifiable part of the verdict-making process in your classroom debates, then you may utilize this additional ballot (see Table 8) to do so, adding its contents to the other three criteria for judgment and thereby raising the total number of points possible in any round from 15 to 20.

Finally, I have included a number of potential questions for student debate. Because four students are involved in any debate round, the following six questions allow for the involvement of all members of a class of 24 students.

Questions for Debate

- Is Hester Prynne ultimately a heroic figure? Make sure to support your argument with textual support, as well as a clear definition of what it means to be a hero.

- Does Dimmesdale's public confession undo or make up for his years of silent guilt and suffering? Make sure to support your argument with evidence from the text.

- Is an understanding of "The Custom-House" a necessary or important part of the experience of reading *The Scarlet Letter*? Support your point of view with sound logic and clear evidence from the text.

- In Chapter III of *The Scarlet Letter*, the mysterious stranger whom we come to know as Roger Chillingworth predicts that Hester's punishment will forever make her "a living sermon against sin" (p. 46). Does Chillingworth's prediction prove true? Make sure to support your argument with clearly supportive details from the text.

TABLE 7
Interteam Debate Ballot

The Scarlet Letter

Date _____   Judge _____

Topic _____

Affirmative Team _____

Negative Team _____

Before allotting to students any points or ranks, or determining the winning team, fill out the following table. Assess the four debaters separately in each category. Do not assign more points in any category than the maximum possible. Then, rank each debater in order of performance (1 for the most successful, 2 for the next highest performer, etc.).

1st Affirmative	2nd Affirmative		1st Negative	2nd Negative
Points:	Points:	Delivery (Pace, Clarity, Tone, Sportsmanship) **5 Pts. Maximum**	Points:	Points:
Reasons Why:	Reasons Why:		Reasons Why:	Reasons Why:
Points:	Points:	Persuasiveness (Organization, Argumentation) **5 Pts. Maximum**	Points:	Points:
Reasons Why:	Reasons Why:		Reasons Why:	Reasons Why:
Points:	Points:	Textual Support (Quotations, Logical Analysis) **5 Pts. Maximum**	Points:	Points:
Reasons Why:	Reasons Why:		Reasons Why:	Reasons Why:

1st Aff. _____   1st Neg. _____

Total Points _____   Rank _____   Total Points _____   Rank _____

2nd Aff. _____   2nd Neg. _____

Total Points _____   Rank _____   Total Points _____   Rank _____

Total Score, Affirmative Team _____   Total Score, Negative Team _____

In my opinion, the better debating was done by the _____, for these reasons:
(Affirmative or Negative)

Signature of Judge _____

TABLE 8
Interteam Debate Sportsmanship Ballot

The Scarlet Letter

Date _____   Judge _____
Topic _____
Affirmative Team _____
Negative Team _____

Please score the four debaters in terms of their portrayal of ethical, sportsmanlike behavior. Consider their delivered speeches, as well as their body language, tones of voice, and general attitudes during the debate.

Sportsmanship Rating	*1st Affirmative Debater*	*1st Negative Debater*	*2nd Affirmative Debater*	*2nd Negative Debater*
5: Outgoing, friendly, civil, and fair throughout the debate				
4: Civil and fair throughout the debate				
3: Civil and fair throughout most of the debate, but bordering on unfriendliness in places				
2: Somewhat civil during part of the debate, but rather unfriendly or combative at certain times				
1: Unfriendly or combative throughout most of the debate, bordering on offensive disrespect				

- Does Hawthorne want his readers to view the Puritan past that he describes in an essentially positive or negative light? Justify your answer with logical analysis and evidence from the text.
- Considering how all of the major characters in the novel end up in Chapter XXIV, is the conclusion of *The Scarlet Letter* a just or otherwise fitting one? Justify your answer with sound logic and details from the text.

Lesson Plan: Alternative Letters

This lesson asks students to investigate versions of *The Scarlet Letter* in other media, including film, stage plays, and contemporary fiction. Focusing on the ways in which Hawthorne's basic plot and themes can be interpreted and reimagined, the lesson aims toward students' heightened understanding of the novel's essential humanity and resultant timelessness. It can be found on pages 138–141.

Conclusion

This chapter contained mechanisms and methods for augmenting your students' understanding of *The Scarlet Letter* by spurring discussion. Chapter 6 contains a number of devices and approaches to writing assignments, including a number of essay types and creative-interpretive projects, as well as accompanying assignment sheets and grading rubrics.

Chapter Materials

Lesson Plan:
Alternative Letters

Purpose/Objective

This lesson is intended to strengthen students' understanding of some reasons and ways in which *The Scarlet Letter* has in popular culture transcended the limits of its own setting and goings-on, having been extrapolated into various forms by a number of writers and other artists, as it shall continue to be for many generations. Moreover, students by the end of this lesson should understand that the reason why *The Scarlet Letter* survives and remains vibrant and relevant in so many artistic media is that at its center are some very common aspects of the human experience.

Placement

This lesson is ideally placed after students conclude their reading of the novel. In order to get as much from the lesson cognitively as possible, and in order to avoid letting any cats out of the bag relative to the conclusion of the book's plot, you should not administer the lesson before the end of your unit.

Warning

Several of the adaptations identified in this lesson plan contain explicit material that is potentially unsuitable for particular students. *The Scarlet Letter* itself is no stranger to controversy, as the story's elements consistently push the boundaries of good taste; the original novel did so at the time of its publication, several of its original film adaptations did so upon release, and there are in fact some modern adaptations of the story about which I felt uncomfortable enough to exclude them from being recommended resources for this lesson. Please use discretion in deciding to administer this activity, and certainly you should preview all materials accessible in the first place.

Materials Required

Students will for this lesson need access to a variety of recorded or printed materials relevant to *The Scarlet Letter*. As it is improbable that any local public library would house all of the associated materials described below, subscriptions or other access to online collections of films and printed materials is recommended. For the secondary creative portion of this lesson, students will need little beyond standard materials required for writing.

Duration

This lesson can be accomplished over the course of four "episodes": a 15-minute introduction to the lesson incorporating steps 1, 2, and 3; a 2-hour period of research that coincides with step 3; an approximately 30-minute period of reporting on and analyzing students' findings, per steps 3 and 4; and finally a flexible amount of time in which students work creatively on their own reimaginings of *The Scarlet Letter*, as described in step 5. Any additional sharing among your students of their creative products would amount to an extra step, and thus extra time, but all told, this lesson can at its shortest be completed over the course of two scholastic days, accounting for a total of 45 minutes of class time, plus two nights' worth of homework.

Lesson Plan

1. *Anticipatory Set*: Choose a popular movie, familiar to most members of your class, that has been clearly influenced by an earlier work of art. Such films or stories often echo their original inspirations, as *The Lion King* echoes *Hamlet*, *10 Things I Hate About You* echoes *The Taming of the Shrew*, and the *Star Wars* films echo Arthurian legend. If your students are not familiar with the original work of art that inspired the popular film, then you may wish to recapitulate briefly the two tales' similar plots. By no means do I recommend that you show either film in its entirety to your class, but rather ask the students themselves to pick out the correlating portions of both stories, thereby constructing a simple table of similarities indicating the direct influence of the original upon the adaptation. You might afterward engage in a brief discussion as to why certain stories continually get reworked and retold in our culture.

2. *Communication of Objective*: After discussing how storytellers often extrapolate central elements from one tale or source in the creation of another, identify as this lesson's objective not only an investigation of other creative works influenced in this way by *The Scarlet Letter*, but also a new creation according to the same influence.

3. *Research and Comparison*: Students will firstly need to familiarize themselves with adaptations of *The Scarlet Letter*, both directly and indirectly. Thus, they should choose from the following chart one item from the column on the left and one item from the column on the right.

LESSON 3

Performed or Adapted Versions of *The Scarlet Letter*	Original Adaptations of a Different Title
1896 opera composed by Walter Damrosch	*Roger's Version* (1986) novel by John Updike
1911 silent film directed by Joseph W. Smiley	*The Holder of the World* (1993) novel by Bharati Mukherjee
1934 American film directed by Robert G. Vignola	*In the Blood* (1999) stage play by Suzan-Lori Parks
1973 German film directed by Wim Wenders	*Easy A* (2010) American film directed by Will Gluck
1979 PBS miniseries directed by Rick Hauser	*When She Woke* (2011) novel by Hillary Jordan
1995 American film directed by Roland Joffé, starring Demi Moore	

Having chosen their two selected adaptations, students should research them for parallels to Hawthorne's original. Online databases, accessible collections of video clips, MP3 music download engines, Google Books, and the like might all prove helpful to students trying to investigate these alternative works. They should, over the course of approximately 2 hours of research, not peruse, but rather sample the plots, styles, and approaches to adaptation taken by both works. Essentially, they should be able to report at the end of their research period what elements of *The Scarlet Letter* were incorporated successfully into the adapted works, what portions of the original were in their or the popular opinions misused or failingly adapted, and what parts of Hawthorne's novel were simply ignored or otherwise left out of the new work. You may want them to present their findings orally to each other or in a traditionally written research essay (or a modification thereof); directions for assigning and evaluating research essays can be found in Chapter 6: Writing About *The Scarlet Letter*, found on pages 143–181.

4. *Commonalities:* After students gather and report their findings, you should ask them collectively to organize into particular categories what they have discovered. This step is particularly relevant to original adaptations of *The Scarlet Letter* produced under different names (i.e., the right side of the chart above). By considering and labeling what portions of the original story are adapted to new trappings (e.g., in 2011's *When She Woke*, the transgressor dyes her skin rather than wear an embroidered

"A," and in 1999's *In the Blood*, the protagonist has five children rather than the singular Pearl, although both she and Hester Prynne are single mothers). Such adaptations can be labeled and collected into categories of story elements that have been altered, including the setting, the socioeconomic circumstances of the characters, the crime, the punishment, and the outcome. What students will discover is that the central themes of guilt, repentance, dread, sinfulness, and self-recreation generally remain intact. Why? These ideas are the most human elements of the novel; the details listed above are to some degree peripheral, and they can be adapted to a variety of settings and circumstances without altering core messages, values, or themes.

5. *Re-Creations:* The final step of this lesson requires that your students themselves engage in the creative process of adaptation by composing original short stories that incorporate the central themes and concept of *The Scarlet Letter*, albeit in distinct situations of their own invention. To be particularly directive, you may require that their original stories incorporate at least three themes of Hawthorne's original, as well as the central development of its plot, but include a completely new protagonist, antagonist(s), crime, punishment, and setting. These stories can then be shared among members of your class as a demonstration of the quite-flexible malleability of Hawthorne's conception.

Closure

Ultimately, what you should desire from your students here is not only an outstanding original literary product, but also a strong understanding of just why *The Scarlet Letter* remains a popular and continually relevant tale on a thematically human level. You may of course conclude the lesson with a brief discussion to this end, which in itself would allow you the opportunity to reinforce for your students several of the theories of literary criticism found in Chapter 2, namely Aristotelianism, Deconstructionism, and Feminism. Information on the 10 critical theories of literary interpretation can be found on pages 13–16.

Chapter 6

Writing About *The Scarlet Letter*

No matter what academic disciplines students gravitate toward in college, no matter what subjects they choose as majors, they will be evaluated in large part based on their abilities to write well. Writing in general and the academic essay in particular constitute the common currency of scholarship all over the world. It is therefore simply our professional responsibility to train students how to write effectively in a variety of styles and formats, which is of course the focus of this particular chapter. Not only for large-scale success in the future, but also more immediately and practically for success on the AP English Literature exam, in this chapter I offer a number of varied writing assignments and assessment instruments, which I hope that you will utilize as suits your needs. Specifically, I here identify, discuss, and provide materials for six divergent types of writing aims and assignments.

 The first writing activity or type upon which I focus is not a full essay at all, but rather a standard paragraph. Per the College Board itself, students should learn firstly to organize and compose well-supported A-E-C (Assertion-Evidence-Commentary) paragraphs before they proceed to longer analyses, so I have included several analytical prompts and questions on reproducible sheets in the Chapter Materials section, all of which can be administered at the culmination of the novel or, perhaps more usefully, as your students proceed through it. The next two of these types I have modeled on the types of writing that students are asked to produce on the Scholastic Aptitude Test and the AP English Literature and Composition Examination. The SAT requires children to write argumentatively and persuasively on a debatable topic; essays of this type are timed to 25 minutes each. The AP English Literature exam, however, asks students to analyze selected short literary works, either excerpted or in their entireties, dissecting their formats, styles, techniques, and literary effects within a span of 40 minutes; essays found on the SAT are argumentative in nature, while such AP essays are expository.

Moreover, at least in undergraduate courses concerning English literature, most essays replicate the analytical nature of these latter AP essays, although in college they are generally much longer and more complex as a rule; thus, college-length literary analyses are here treated as a distinct genre of composition. Research-based writing, additionally, is a fifth unique type, requiring that students engage in individualized research, synthesize their findings, and present them to an audience of some sort (even an audience composed of one lone professor); that being said, students' presentations of their research findings oftentimes do not take the form of composed text, as a growing number of professors in disparate academic disciplines favor engaging in-class oral presentations over the traditional academic essay. As a sixth type of responsive product, an assignment requiring students to interpret, reframe, and reproduce in original ways a thematic aspect (or several) of a literary work is here presented as a creative alternative, requiring advanced learners' abilities to meld real-world, potentially modern issues with "big picture" aspects of fictional literature. Taken wholly, the six writing styles considered in this chapter constitute a diverse smorgasbord of opportunities to harness students' creative, reflective, and responsive potentials.

Paragraph Completion: Assertion, Evidence, and Commentary

Just as children must learn to walk before they can run, student writers must first master the basic skills of persuasion before they can compose effective argumentative or analytical essays. The most basic of these persuasive abilities involves the explanation of evidence. Like any kind of effective writers, students must do more than simply present supportive facts and details; they must be able to explain their significance to a basic point of view. The accompanying paragraph composition worksheets, found on pages 168–176, have been designed with just this ability in sight.

It is no secret that an effective, albeit basic, body paragraph in any kind of argumentative or analytical essay contains what some teachers call a "quote sandwich," namely a piece of evidence or example centered within a topic sentence at the top and further explanation or elaboration at the bottom. Probably a more common name for this paragraph structure comes from the College Board itself: the A-E-C paragraph, an acronym outlining effective paragraphs' inclusion of an assertion (A) or topic sentence, evidence (E) supporting that assertion, and commentary (C) upon that evidence, explaining its relevance to the initial topic or assertion of the paragraph. This formulaic structure is no secret among teachers of gifted and advanced students, surely, but it is perhaps dismissed as elementary or relegated to a proverbial backseat because of admittedly legitimate time constraints. Nevertheless, students of all ages and abilities must *have* the building blocks of strong argumentation before they use them to construct.

With this fact in mind, I have included in the Chapter Materials section a number of practice materials requiring students to compose A-E-C paragraphs based on simple writing prompts and bounded within particular series of chapters. In order to allow you, if you wish, to utilize in your classroom the worksheets as de facto reading quizzes after nightly homework assignments, I have intentionally focused them upon commonly grouped series of chapters, as well as attempted to eliminate most context clues from the prompts themselves, thus requiring students' genuine understanding and reasoned commentary upon what they may have studied the night beforehand.

As with any writing assignment, also, you may find it useful to model successful or unsuccessful responses with your class after each attempt at the composition of an effective A-E-C paragraph. Submissions can be graded simply on a 4-point criterion-based scale—requiring the inclusion of four parts: an assertion statement, evidence, commentary, and decently effective grammar and punctuation—or you may modify and utilize one of the other grading rubrics contained in this book to assess these paragraphs. Regardless, I personally believe that the dividends paid on the AP English Literature exam as a result of structured, consistent practice in composing basic, yet effective, body paragraphs will certainly prove valuable in the end, and I therefore encourage you to use the enclosed A-E-C worksheets as you see fit in your own classroom.

25-Minute Argumentative SAT-Style Essays

The essay portion of the College Board's Scholastic Aptitude Test, introduced roughly a decade ago, requires test-takers to consider, take, and support positions on debatable issues, though perhaps not controversially so. Essay prompts formulaically ask students to consider an open-ended issue, and the test allows 25 minutes in which each student must compose one well-organized, strongly supported response to the issue. The College Board makes available a great number of sample SAT questions and official grading rubrics, plus sets of hierarchically taxonomical anchor papers that evaluators, be they teachers or parents, can use to gauge their effectiveness in assessing students' essays.

Whether standardized test preparation is a contractually expected or even a worthwhile part of any professional educator's job is a rather hot-button issue. On the one hand, there is value, of course, in training students to succeed on the SAT, a singular psychometric instrument holding much sway over the college choices available to high school graduates; on the other hand, "teaching to the test" as either a curricular goal or a pedagogical technique suffers a poor reputation among educators who consider aptitude tests extraneous to the disciplined academics of high school. To paraphrase simply the thoughts of a given high school teacher, I teach English literature, not test-taking, and the SAT is not part of my curriculum. A legitimate point of view, perhaps yes, but the focused, argumentative, substantiated, on-the-spot type of writing that students must produce for the SAT does demand valuable compositional skills. Preparing students for the SAT essay portion, therefore, is probably not akin to putting the proverbial cart before the horse, as some teachers may complain; more clearly, it may just be an altogether separate horse than the one harnessed in traditional literature courses.

To the point, the argumentative essay is a different beast altogether than the literary exegesis and the common book report. Convincing, well-supported argumentation, especially within an amount of time as limiting as 25 minutes, requires students to think quickly, to organize logically, and to compose proficiently, utilizing the support of sources that may or may not qualify as canonical literature, but that certainly uphold a student's position on a given essay topic. To write an effective argumentative essay in 25 minutes is just plain hard, a fact that perhaps helps to validate the outcome of this portion of the SAT, and the time management skills required for success on this task are themselves skills to be learned or improved through repeated practice.

For all of the above reasons, I here offer a number of writing prompts and questions that aim to enrich your students' persuasive and argumentative faculties. If you wish to reproduce the SAT's demanding time constraints in your classroom, then limit your class's composition time to 25 minutes. As a general rule, also, it will probably prove useful, prior to administering any writing assignment, to model for your class sample questions and responses, such as graded anchor papers, interpreting as a group what does and does not make a successful essay of this type.

Sample Questions

- In "The Custom-House: Introductory to *The Scarlet Letter*," Hawthorne implies a great distaste for longstanding governmental bureaucrats, suggesting their nepotism, laziness, and inefficiency. Do you agree with Hawthorne's implication that individuals should hold governmental jobs, even in appointed positions, for strictly limited amounts of time? Organize and compose an essay in which you consider this issue. Support your argument with examples academic or otherwise.

- In Chapter 2 of *The Scarlet Letter*, Hawthorne states that for Puritan Bostonians, "religion and law were almost identical" (p. 37). Do you believe that religious principles should be the central focuses of political law? Organize and compose an essay in which you consider this issue. Support your argument with examples academic or otherwise.

- The inciting crime of *The Scarlet Letter* is of course both a religious and a civic one, and as punishment for it, Hester Prynne is forced to bear a marking that she cannot shed. Do you believe that some wrongdoings are so bad that their committers should never be forgiven, but forever branded in society? Organize and compose an essay in which you consider this issue. Support your argument with examples academic or otherwise.

- Part of Hawthorne's wordplay in *The Scarlet Letter* arises from characters' names. For example, both Chillingworth and Dimmesdale have character traits implied connotatively from their surnames. Do you believe that people's names are arbitrarily given and thus ultimately meaningless, or can we actually discern aspects of each other from our given names? Organize and compose an essay in which you consider this issue. Support your argument with examples academic or otherwise.

- In Chapter 15 of *The Scarlet Letter*, Hester says of her former husband Chillingworth, "He has done me worse wrong than I did him!" (p. 114). Dimmesdale echoes her comment several chapters later in saying, "That old man's revenge has been blacker than my sin" (p. 125). Both of these statements imply the point of view that while the initial commission of crime may be horrible, the search for retribution against a criminal is somehow even worse. Do you agree with this perspective? Organize and compose an essay in which you consider this issue. Support your argument with examples academic or otherwise.

- Near the conclusion of *The Scarlet Letter*, Hester Prynne and Arthur Dimmesdale resolve to abandon their posts in the New World and return to Europe. Effectively, they choose flight over fight. Ironically, in the novel's de facto epilogue, Hester returns from Europe to her old residence in Boston. When faced with difficulties of a cultural or societal nature, rather than with strictly interpersonal conflicts, is it sometimes the most prudent reaction simply to leave? Organize and compose an essay in which you consider this issue. Support your argument with examples academic or otherwise.

Grading Rubric

Students' engagement in any writing process of course produces only half of their potential gains, for without a teacher's prompt provision to them of useful feedback, students' improvements are hardly optimized. The reproducible page found in Table 9 is an original grading rubric that I constructed to parallel the College Board's own expectations for students' products on the essay portion of the SAT. Thus, as they would likewise be for the College Board itself, your students' products are here gauged on a 6-point scale.

You may find it valuable to initiate a peer-assessment process among members of your class, whereby they "grade" each others' argumentative essays using this very rubric. Please note, though, that such peer assessment is by and large invalid if students are not trained prior to engaging in the activity as to how the rubric "works" and what essays of various grades actually contain and "look like"; thus, anticipatory modeling of scored anchor papers with your class is strongly recommended. Moreover, it is perhaps both prudent and sensitive to implement peer assessment on an identity-blind basis, whereby essays are photocopied, minus their authors' names, prior to the peer-evaluation process.

40-Minute Analytical AP-Style Essays

The AP English Literature and Composition Examination involves students' composition of three different essays, in addition to successful handling of a battery of multiple-choice questions on numerous literary excerpts. Distinct from the argumentative essays required by the SAT, these three essays are analytical, spurring students to scrutinize the effects, purposes, themes, and the like of several creative works of literature. To succeed, students must be literary scientists of sorts, able to dissect texts—one excerpt of poetry, another of prose, and a work of choice—for themes, symbols, syntactical and otherwise structural aspects, key diction, and similarly creative brushstrokes. Students' training in literary devices and compositional techniques, as well as in the 10 critical perspectives upon literature found in Chapter 2 of this book, is solid diagnostic preparation.

Analytical essays of this type must be organized just as well as the argumentative sort required by the SAT, but these analyses must also be supported by precise details, namely quotations and descriptions of features taken from intricate readings of the offered literary selections. Additionally, these AP-style essays should as a rule be longer and better-executed than their SAT-style counterparts, for students are allowed nearly twice as long to write these analyses as they are to compose argumentatively for the SAT: 40 minutes as opposed to 25, respectively. Once again, please note that the College Board has released to the public numerous AP essay prompts, selections, and questions, as well as actual students' responses to them, all taken fully from English Literature and Composition exams; thus, sharing with your class a number of College Board-scored anchor papers is likewise suggested preparation for students' engagement with essays of this type.

TABLE 9
Grading Rubric for 25-Minute SAT-Style Essays

	Grade of 6	*Grade of 5*	*Grade of 4*
Overall Impression	An exceptional composition, indicating obvious and even mastery	A successful composition, indicating reasonably even mastery	A capable composition, indicating sufficient mastery
Essayist's Point of View	Sharply discerning point of view	Able and perceptive point of view	Lucid point of view
Support for Position/ Argument	Obviously suitable examples, reasons, and evidence are used	Suitable examples, reasons, and evidence are used	Sufficient examples, reasons, and evidence are used
Organization and Focus	Excellent organization and focus	Solid organization and focus	Coherent organization and acceptable focus
Progression of Ideas	Skillful progression of ideas	Articulate progression of ideas	Reasonable progression of ideas
Usage of Vocabulary	An apparently practiced and exact use of varied vocabulary	Appropriately varied vocabulary	Acceptable but inconsistent use of varied vocabulary
Sentence Structure	A significant and expressive range of sentence structures	A range of sentence structures	A limited range of sentence structures
Grammar, Usage, and Mechanics	Free of all major and minor errors	Nearly free of errors	A number of errors exist
	Grade of 3	*Grade of 2*	*Grade of 1*
Overall Impression	An inadequate composition, indicating emergent mastery	A highly inadequate composition, indicating slight mastery	An essentially deficient composition, indicating little or no mastery
Essayist's Point of View	Apparent point of view	Unclear point of view	No viable point of view
Support for Position/ Argument	Insufficient examples, reasons, and evidence are used	Poorly chosen examples, reasons, and evidence are used	Few or no examples, reasons, and evidence are used
Organization and Focus	Limited organization and focus	Poor organization and focus	Disorganized and unfocused
Progression of Ideas	Some faults are present in the progression of ideas	Highly faulty progression of ideas	Disorderly or unintelligible progression of ideas
Usage of Vocabulary	Pedestrian and somewhat incorrect use of vocabulary	Inadequate and often incorrect use of vocabulary	Elementary errors in vocabulary
Sentence Structure	No range of sentence structures	Widespread difficulties in sentence structure	Extreme errors in sentence structure
Grammar, Usage, and Mechanics	Frequent errors exist	Major errors confuse the essayist's point in places	Widespread, serious errors greatly interfere with the essayist's point

Teachers are wise to predict that the literary selections found on their students' AP Literature and Composition Examination will be unfamiliar ones, for while it is technically possible that the College Board asks students to analyze works as common as "The Road Not Taken" and "Jabberwocky," it is by and large improbable. Therefore, students should prepare for the test with analytical, compositional, *and* time-management practice, as all three skills will be abundantly required during a 2-hour block of time in which test-takers write three different analyses in response to three very different prompts. The process in which students engage here is different, but no less difficult, than the method by which they write argumentatively for the SAT, so practice and constructive feedback from teachers are critical to students' improvement and eventual success on the AP exam.

For your use in preparing your students for that success, I have designed and included five sample AP-style essay prompts in this chapter's materials section (see pp. 177–181), each excerpted from a particular section of *The Scarlet Letter*. As the five different essay prompts focus upon distinct selections and analytical topics, students who compose all of them will gain from exposure to a number of different techniques, devices, and purposes, each of which is reasonably to be expected on the actual AP Literature and Composition Examination.

Grading Rubric

As with all writing assignments, students' improvement in composing successful timed essays is aided by prompt, focused feedback. The grading rubric found in Table 10, which mirrors the College Board's expectations for essays written for the AP English Literature and Composition exam, is designed to assist your delivery of such feedback. It assesses students' products on a 9-point scale, as does the College Board's own grading instrument for the AP exam, and considers a range of compositional facets.

Once again, students' peer assessment of their classmates' written products can strongly aid in your class's preparation for the AP Literature exam. However, please note that the legitimacy of peer assessment as a teaching device lessens if you do not train your class beforehand on proper use of the rubric and comparative analysis of anchor papers, which helps to ensure that your students understand not only the rubric's evaluative criteria, but also how to assess accurately their classmates' written responses using the instrument. I encourage you here, as I also did with argumentative SAT-style responses, to utilize peer assessment on an identity-blind basis, removing students' names from essays that are shared among members of your class.

TABLE 10
Grading Rubric for AP-Style 40-Minute Essays

Score of 9	Score of 8	Score of 7
• Rhetorical and stylistic devices analyzed correctly with precision *or* • Persuasive argument is cogent, convincing, and well supported	• Rhetorical and stylistic devices analyzed well *or* • Persuasive argument is cogent and convincing, but only somewhat supported	• Rhetorical and stylistic devices analyzed competently *or* • Persuasive argument is cogent, but a lack of development or support is somewhat unconvincing
• Frequent, succinct, and appropriate references to the text, either directly or indirectly	• Some appropriate references to the text, either directly or indirectly	• A few appropriate references to the text, either directly or indirectly
• Point of view is clearly articulated and reinforced extremely well	• Point of view is clearly articulated and reinforced appropriately	• Point of view is clearly articulated, but reinforced only somewhat
• Extremely well written...any existent errors are inconsequential	• Well written...very few and only minor errors are made	• Some errors exist, but they do not interfere with the writer's clear expression of ideas
Score of 6	**Score of 5**	**Score of 4**
• Rhetorical and stylistic devices analyzed somewhat haphazardly *or* • Underdeveloped and undersupported persuasive argument is only slightly convincing	• Relevant rhetorical and stylistic devices are analyzed very little *or* • Persuasive argument is underdeveloped and undersupported, and thus unconvincing	• Only secondary rhetorical and stylistic devices are analyzed *or* • Persuasive argument is superficial, perhaps missing the point of the question/prompt
• A few references to the text, directly or indirectly, are only somewhat relevant	• The writer refers to the text, directly or indirectly, very little, and only somewhat relevantly	• Almost no relevant references to the text are made, either directly or indirectly
• Point of view is vaguely articulated and reinforced only somewhat	• Point of view is vaguely articulated and reinforced hardly at all	• Point of view is developed incoherently and only somewhat clear
• Errors exist, very few of which are serious enough to interfere with the writer's clear expression	• Errors in diction, syntax, or grammar interfere with the writer's clear expression of ideas	• Immature errors exist, demonstrating the writer's lack of control over diction and syntax
Score of 3	**Score of 2**	**Score of 1**
• Secondary rhetorical and stylistic devices are incorrectly analyzed *or* • Persuasive argument is seriously flawed, as well as mostly off the topic of the question/prompt	• Any attempted analysis of rhetorical or stylistic devices is extremely simplistic *or* • Persuasive argument is seriously flawed, irrelevant, and unorganized	• No attempt is made to analyze rhetorical or stylistic devices *or* • Irrelevant persuasive argument is excessively flawed and extremely unorganized
• No direct references to the text are made, and indirect references are mostly irrelevant	• No relevant references to the text are made, either directly or indirectly	• No references to the text are made at all, either directly or indirectly
• The writer's point of view is unclear and disjointed	• The writer's point of view is expressed quite unclearly	• The writer's point of view is incomprehensible
• Very immature errors exist, demonstrating the writer's lack of control over standard English syntax and grammar	• Overly simplistic errors demonstrate the writer's lack of control over basic English diction, syntax, and grammar	• Overwhelming errors indicate the writer's extreme lack of control over basic English diction, syntax, and grammar

Scores of 0 are given for blank papers, simple paraphrases of prompts, or essays not on assigned topics.

Extended College-Length Analytical Essays

Say the phrase "English paper" to most high-achieving high school and college students and graduates, and slight variations on one image probably emerge from their recollections: a long exposition of the themes, symbolism, or cultural import of a given novel or poem, probably measured between 6–10 pages and including numerous quotations, citations, and references or works cited at its back. I do not mean to say that these legions of hypothetical students are wrong in their imaginings. Indeed, such lengthy written products are more than common in English courses, especially at undergraduate and graduate levels of literary study, where, in many cases, they constitute the majority of students' final grades. The long analytical essay is, after all, the lingua franca of English majors, is it not?

On this note, the College Board as an academically legislative body requires that teachers of AP courses in all disciplines dispense to their students legitimately collegiate instruction; this is the reason why so many undergraduate institutions offer incoming freshmen credit for the passage of AP exams. The College Board upholds this standard, in fact, by approving or denying individual teachers' unique course syllabi in order to monitor consistent rigor and vet appropriate approaches to literary study. We AP teachers are truly expected to be pseudo-college professors, so we would be remiss to ignore college-length analytical essays in favor of shorter, timed, in-class prompts aimed solely at higher scores on the AP test. Yes, students' performances on the English Literature exam ultimately determine their potential reception of college credit, but it is no less critical—and incumbent upon us to ensure—that once they actually matriculate to college they are familiar with the procedure and experience of writing 8-page papers, not just five-paragraph handwritten essays, as required by the AP exam. As stated previously in this chapter, these two types of essays really are two different beasts and should be treated as such.

When assigning to my own AP students such long analytical papers, rather than ask of them open-ended interpretive questions resulting in loosely bounded essays on topics of their choice (e.g., "write a paper somehow analyzing the symbolism of *The Scarlet Letter*"), I give to them a closed list of possible essay theses—yes, I write the theses myself—allowing each student to choose whichever thesis and position he or she wishes to defend and requiring him or her to include it, word for word, in the submitted essay. This approach greatly lessens students' potential to discover a useable, plagiarize-able essay elsewhere, for the likelihood of other people having not only written, but also published a legitimate essay on the precise topic chosen from my list is remote.

Here is a list of such potential theses concerning *The Scarlet Letter*. You may wish to assign them to your students as a "menu of choices" from which students can "pick their poison," so to speak. Additionally, you may wish to enact the safeguard against formatting trickery which I utilize in my own class, namely suggesting essays' lengths not in terms of their numbers of total pages, but rather in terms of their aggregate word counts. On most word processing software, writers are easily able to adjust contents, and thus the numbers, of computerized pages by altering font and margin sizes, which proves impossible if students need to produce a set number of words instead of a set number of pages. To wit, it is far easier to monkey with formatting in order to turn 5 pages into 7 than to turn 1,000 words into 1,500. Simply consider the fact that an average page typed in a standard size and font, bounded on all sides by one-inch margins, contains approximately 250 to 300 words, and you can easily estimate the length of essay for which you are hoping from your students.

Sample Essay Theses

- In "The Custom-House: Introductory to *The Scarlet Letter*," Hawthorne suggests his disdain for bureaucratic government, citing his colleagues' nepotism and inefficiency, but evidence otherwise exists to suggest that Hawthorne's displeasure actually stems not from his consideration of others, but rather from his own senses of shame and dissatisfaction with himself.

- In contrast to implications of "The Custom-House: Introductory to *The Scarlet Letter*," Hawthorne throughout *The Scarlet Letter* demonstrates that Puritanical New England is actually less purely successful of a society than his own 19th century culture.

- Throughout *The Scarlet Letter*, Hawthorne utilizes the rose and the brook as natural symbols that underscore his thematic commentary upon purity and corruption.

- Although female characters are fully absent from "The Custom-House: Introductory to *The Scarlet Letter*" and portrayed unflatteringly in *The Scarlet Letter*'s earliest chapters, Hawthorne's depictions of women evolve throughout the novel, which proves at its conclusion to be a strongly feminist work.

- Hawthorne in *The Scarlet Letter* utilizes emotionally connotative diction and vivid imagery to engender Roger Chillingworth's dynamic transformation from a sympathetic character to a villainous one, effectively swapping places with Hester Prynne in the novel's antagonistic hierarchy.

- Unlike the city of Boston, the forest is paradoxically portrayed in *The Scarlet Letter* as a place both of danger and of truth.

- Through his utilization of connotative diction, allusion, and omniscient narration, Hawthorne by the end of *The Scarlet Letter* suggests that Roger Chillingworth quite clearly transfigures himself into a devilish character.
- Hawthorne throughout *The Scarlet Letter* conveys his general dislike for and lack of trust in institutionalized bodies of people, in contrast to his ultimate faith in and hope for individual human beings.
- The central objectified symbol of *The Scarlet Letter* is not Hester's scarlet A itself, but rather the scaffold in the marketplace's center, which grows in figurative import as the novel progresses toward and reaches its conclusion.

Grading Rubric

I evaluate my own students' college-length literary analyses using the rubric found on page 155, which both highlights and requires specific compositional elements, as any rubric does, and proves flexible enough to allow some of the holistic assessment common in many undergraduate English seminars. In other words, although I focus upon particular skills and requirements in this instrument, I also allow you some wiggle room to evaluate essays based on your overall impression of them.

Submissions and Returns

It is my own pedagogical belief that the more ways I can somehow transform summative assessment into formative assessment, helping pupils to learn even as they are being assessed, the better. The short time that I am given to work with students is maximized if I am able to find ways to turn even tests into learning experiences. Thus, in my own classes I attempt to add educational value to two mundane procedures necessary to the assignment and evaluation of long essays: my collection of students' papers and, after grading, my redistribution of the analyses back to their student authors.

As to the first, on due dates, when essays are collected, many teachers simply cap the writing process by quickly collecting papers, then moving on without much ado to the next activity or unit, leaving the essays themselves forgotten or ignored by the class—one more hoop through which they had to jump on their way toward graduation—until they are someday returned with grades and feedback. To me, such a collection procedure is just anticlimactic and thus unsatisfying. I believe that students who work hard to produce such long essays should be provided a sense of closure or culmination greater than that generated by an expedient passing of papers to the front of the classroom; we teachers want students to feel proud of their work, which in my mind is part and parcel of a sharing of it with classmates. After all, extrinsic motivation for praise is a powerful human motivator.

Name: _____ Date: _____

Scoring Rubric for Extended Analytical Essays

A + (90–100 points)	B + (80–90 points)	C + (70–80 points)	D + (60–70 points)	F + (below 60 points)
Essays earning grades of "A" are outstanding in their clear and consistent mastery of analytical skills, demonstrating their writers' exceptional control of effective writing techniques, sustaining extremely insightful and in-depth analysis of complex ideas, and developing and supporting their main points with logically compelling scrutiny and highly persuasive examples. Such essays are clear, interesting, and correct, including strong and highly effective introductory and conclusive paragraphs, as well as appropriate transitions both within paragraphs and across the entire piece. They are sharply focused and well organized, demonstrating coherent unity and a smooth analytical progression, as well as referring frequently and carefully to the text, both directly and indirectly. These essays display excellent use of language, highlighted by effective sentence variety and precisely apt vocabulary; they demonstrate their authors' superior facility with sentence structure, grammar, usage, and mechanics, including few, if any, errors.	Essays earning grades of "B" are effective in their clear and reasonably consistent mastery of analytical skills, demonstrating their writers' considerable control of effective writing techniques, sustaining generally insightful analysis of complex ideas, and developing and supporting their main points with logically sound scrutiny and well-chosen, appropriate examples. Such essays are clear, interesting, and mostly correct, including skillful and effective introductory and conclusive paragraphs, as well as transitions that are generally appropriate and relatively widespread throughout the piece. They are clearly focused and well organized, demonstrating good overall coherence and an apparent analytical progression, as well as referring frequently to the text, both directly and indirectly. These essays display fluent use of language, highlighted by generally effective sentence variety and appropriate vocabulary; they demonstrate their authors' good control of sentence structure, grammar, usage, and mechanics, including occasional, though not overly numerous, errors.	Essays earning grades of "C" are competent in their fairly clear and developing mastery of analytical skills, demonstrating their writers' adequate control of effective writing techniques, sustaining relevant analysis of important ideas, and supporting their main points with acceptable inquiry and sufficient examples. Such essays are reasonably clear and mostly correct, including satisfactory introductory and conclusive paragraphs, as well as occasional usages of appropriate transitions. They are passably focused and organized, demonstrating reasonable coherence and a sufficient analytical progression, as well as referring commonly to the text, either directly or indirectly. These essays display adequate use of language to convey meaning, including some sentence variety and generally appropriate vocabulary; they demonstrate their authors' satisfactory control of sentence structure, grammar, usage, and mechanics, including frequent errors, very few of which are simplistic in nature.	Essays earning grades of "D" are inadequate, revealing limited mastery of analytical skills, demonstrating their writers' inconsistent control of effective writing techniques, sustaining weak analysis of important ideas, and addressing relatively unsupported main points with brittle inquiry and insufficient examples. Such essays are superficial, though mostly correct, and include cursory introductory and conclusive paragraphs, as well as few, if any, appropriate transitions. They are disjointedly focused and organized, demonstrating the writer's overall inability to compose coherently and logically, as well as referring vaguely and indirectly to the text. These essays display weak use of language to convey meaning, including little sentence variety and commonly awkward vocabulary; they demonstrate their authors' unsatisfactory control of sentence structure, grammar, usage, and mechanics, including widespread errors, some of which are simplistic in nature.	Essays earning grades of "F" are seriously flawed or limited, revealing very little mastery of analytical skills, demonstrating their writers' lack of control of effective writing techniques, sustaining seriously flawed analysis of important ideas, and addressing main points without support or examples. Such essays are simple and in many ways incorrect, including little or no introductory and conclusive paragraphs, as well as very few appropriate transitions. They are disorganized and/or unfocused, demonstrating the writer's fundamental inability to compose coherently and logically, as well as exhibiting an almost total neglect of reference to the text. These essays display deficient use of language to convey meaning, including almost no sentence variety and highly awkward vocabulary in many places; they demonstrate their authors' inadequate control of sentence structure, grammar, usage, and mechanics, including pervasive errors, many of which are simplistic in nature.

Total Points (out of 100): _____

> ### Procedural Directions for Essay Submissions
>
> 1. Carefully checking that all of your pages are in the correct order, please staple your essay, then place and leave it on top of your desk.
> 2. Please stand up, move about the classroom, and choose an essay to read; do so carefully, thoroughly, and silently. When you are finished reading that essay, please return it to the author's desk and choose another to read similarly.
> 3. I am going to collect the essays "permanently" in 30 minutes. You have that amount of time not only to read as many peers' essays as possible, but to edit your own in any way that you wish. If you want to add or amend anything to/in your essay, then please do so in pen. I shall read and grade any such additions or amendments as if they were included, typed, as original portions of your essay. Keep in mind, please, that while you may add anything to your essay at all, from quotations to extra sentences of explanation, from extra transitions to formatting minutiae, I am going to grade all such insertions exactly as I would any other portion of your typed analysis (i.e., watch your grammar, punctuation, spelling, etc.).
> 4. Make sure (e.g., through the usage of arrows) that I can tell easily where each insertion is supposed to go in your text. If you do not wish to make any changes to your essay, of course, then you need not. You have 30 minutes.
>
> ***Figure 2.*** Instructions for peer editing procedures during essay submission process.

For this reason, I ask my own AP students when submitting essays not just to pass around and read each others' work before submission, but also to modify their own essays as they gain from their classmates' products ideas of how their own papers might be improved. Consider that many teachers ask their classes to engage in peer editing as an evaluative tool, encouraging students to find and correct mistakes in their peers' essays. Truth be told, students' motivation for performing well as they do so is low; especially after a presumably late night spent writing their own essays, the opportunity to nitpick grammatical and stylistic errors from friends' papers is hardly an incentive for which they wait anxiously, especially when there is little personal benefit to be gained from doing well on this exercise.

Rather than encourage peer editing as an evaluative activity, in my classes I utilize it as a creative one. Figure 2 contains formal instructions for students on how to engage in "peer editing" as they improve and submit their own essays. My usage of this technique in AP classes has been both positive and productive, raising students' motivation to read each others' essays, improving their focus on the task greatly, and allowing them one last opportunity each essay assignment to polish it slightly before submission. You may wish to distribute these directions to your own students, or to reproduce them on the classroom board, the next time that they submit college-length essays.

Additionally, it is human nature, I believe, when receiving back from a teacher any kind of graded work, to look immediately at the score received, then probably to file the assignment away, reading in the case of an essay few if any of the teacher's comments scattered throughout. After all, if a student is happy with the grade received, then why bother reading the comments? On the other hand, if disappointed or upset by the grade, then why should a student disgustedly rehash the reasons for that perceived "failure" to achieve? This is my own opinion, but either way, in terms of both reactions, our efforts as teachers who spend time and take care in commenting upon students' essays largely go wasted.

As one of those stereotypical English teachers who edit and comment upon students' essays extensively, feeling it somewhat of a professional duty to point out every comma splice and split infinitive, I want my students *to read* the notes and markings that I make; after all, I do not like wasting my own time and effort more than students like to waste theirs. To this end, I utilize two procedures to encourage students to read my feedback on their essays. Firstly, I do not offer any numerical grades when I redistribute to them their marked-up papers. Rather than attach my rubric and final grade to a pupil's essay, I hold them back for a day; my students, in turning to the back page anticipatively, are left puzzling, "Where's the grade?" Their immediate and natural impulse to find and compare numbers is preempted, and in my experience they instead peruse my marked-up pages of notes, searching for clues as to how their respective essays were graded. On the next day I give them the rubrics and numerical scores, allowing them at least one evening to consider and digest my comments and suggestions.

Afterward, because I spend so much time in marking and correcting students' grammatical errors, I reward the pupils for after-the-fact editorial work. As Figure 3 indicates, students who identify and correct several errors that they made repeatedly in a given essay are rewarded with a grade bump after the fact. The procedure outlined by Figure 3 is fairly self-explanatory, and I invite you to utilize it in your own classes.

Research Projects and Essays

The process of designing, engaging in, and presenting original research is another important experience preparing students for work beyond high school. College professors nationwide, in all academic disciplines, expect and, to some degree, rely upon incoming students' familiarity with the research process, as well

> # Do You Want 2 Points Added Immediately to the Total Score of Your Essay?
>
> 1. Find two grammatical errors that you commit very commonly in your essay (you must commit each error a minimum of three times to qualify as "very common").
> 2. Complete, type or handwrite, and submit to me the following four sentences by tomorrow:
>
>> One of my most common errors is [name or precise explanation of error], which can be found [first location of error, including a complete description of it], as well as [second location of error, including a complete description of it] and [third location of error, including a complete description of it].
>> I plan to avoid making this error on my next essay by [explanation of tactic].
>>
>> Another of my most common errors is [name or explanation of error], which can be found [first location of error, including a complete description of it], as well as [second location of error, including a complete description of it] and [third location of error, including a complete description of it].
>> I plan to avoid making this error on my next essay by [explanation of tactic].
>>
>> *(There is no need to underline all of your insertions when you type these sentences; it is simply done so here for editorial purposes.)*
>
> 3. No more steps, actually. I shall add 2 points to the total grade for your essay.
>
> ***Figure 3.*** Instructions for garnering additional points on essays through retroactive editing.

as their proficiency in presenting their findings clearly, via writing and otherwise. For traditional scholastic research papers, the rubric used for the assessment of college-level literary analyses, found on p. 161, can be legitimately utilized here as well. Please note, though, that research essays of this style are far more documentary than they are interpretive, so the rubric's emphasis on persuasion and analysis should be tempered somewhat as applied to research papers.

You may, on the other hand, prefer more engaging, creative in-class presentations of students' research findings over traditional essays. Allowing your students opportunities to express their thoughts and to reflect in numerous different ways is good professional practice, I feel, for "assessment variety" encourages students' development of fuller academic faculties; to analogize, cooks who have only ever worked with vegetables may prove incapable of preparing tuna correctly, perhaps to their own detriment. In other words, for students used to writing traditional essays, creating and exhibiting instead a visual and oral presentation may just help him or her to develop important abilities rarely accessed in traditional academia.

Here, therefore, are some topics of plausible research created with such presentations, oral or otherwise, in mind. These assignments may all be modified slightly, of course, in order to generate more traditional essay products.

Sample Research Projects

- In the early 19th century, the Reverend Joseph B. Felt published a two-volume history of Salem, MA, entitled *The Annals of Salem* (1827–1828). In this text, he considers, among other things, various laws that were enacted during and shortly after the town's founding. He cites a law passed on May 5, 1694, that seems in retrospect to have greatly influenced Hawthorne's story. Research this particular law, paying attention especially to its apparent genesis and goal, and communicate to your classmates in a well-structured presentation its evident relevance to *The Scarlet Letter*.

- Among the most famous and influential of New England writers prior to Hawthorne himself were two sermonizing ministers, Cotton Mather and Jonathan Edwards. Their most famous individual literary works—*The Wonders of the Invisible World* and "Sinners in the Hands of an Angry God," respectively—portray relationships among human beings, their Christian God, and other supernatural beings. Research these two specific literary sources, determining not only what portions of their contents relate to the story told in *The Scarlet Letter*, but also what aspects of their writing styles potentially influenced Nathaniel Hawthorne, who most certainly read both works. Communicate your findings in a well-documented presentation to your classmates.

- During the early 1840s, Hawthorne undertook to participate in experiences that to some degree influenced not only his own person, but larger intellectual currents in the American Northeast. Research Hawthorne's involvement with the Brook Farm, as well as his subsequent occupation of Concord's Old Manse and friendships with local Transcendentalist writers. Keeping in mind that these particular experiences preceded his employment at Salem's Custom House, as described in "The Custom-House: Introductory to *The Scarlet Letter*," how might they have influenced both Hawthorne's worldly philosophies and his creation of *The Scarlet Letter*? Communicate your findings and conclusions in a well-developed presentation.

- Throughout *The Scarlet Letter*, Hawthorne interjects allusions to various historical personages, events, and customs. Among the earliest of these allusions is his reference in Chapter 1 to "the sainted Ann Hutchinson [who] entered the prison-door" just as Hester Prynne herself does. Some interpreters believe that Hawthorne began his novel with this comparison because he wants us as readers to equate the two women, while others believe that Hawthorne's intention was for our consideration of Hutchinson and Prynne as foils. Research the life and accomplishments of Ann Hutchinson. What parallels exist between her and Hester Prynne, and what do you believe was Hawthorne's intention for making this early comparison? In a multimedia presentation, including quotations from *The Scarlet Letter* and evidence from your research, communicate your findings and point of view.

The Scarlet Letter is perhaps unique among American literary masterpieces because of its clear depiction of two distinct periods of American political history: the age of Puritan colonialism in the Northeast United States and the later antebellum period of established government described in "The Custom-House: Introductory to *The Scarlet Letter*." Choose one of these two periods of United States history and research its political track, including important governmental leaders, civic movements both successful and failed, influences upon our politics both from other nations and from nonpoliticians such as philosophers, and common governmental and otherwise civic events of the time period. Portraying your findings as a social and municipal background to either the action of *The Scarlet Letter* or the later cradle of the tale's imagining and composition, present to your classmates your findings in a well-documented manner.

Grading Rubric

In Table 11, you will find a grading rubric that may be used to evaluate students' research presentations. This rubric's fourth criterion, Adherence to Project Parameters, considers predetermined restrictions such as time limits, which are, of course, malleable according to your instructional purposes and the abilities of your own students. Additionally, this rubric calculates students' performances on a 16-point scale, so to adapt the overall value to a 100-point grading scale, simply multiply students' scores by 6.25.

Individualized Creative-Interpretive Projects

Among the strongest of my own educational beliefs is the idea that the most enduring, most personal, and therefore most valuable growth accomplished by students in school arises not in some kind of academic vacuum, but rather in a creative fusion of scholastic theory and real-world significance. Humans in general

TABLE 11
Grading Rubric for Student's Research Presentations

	4	3	2	1
Content	The project's content is totally legitimate and highly detailed, exhibiting a strong research base.	The project's content is legitimate and detailed, though not exceedingly deep, exhibiting a solid research base.	The project's content is mostly legitimate, but less detailed overall, exhibiting solid research in only some areas.	The project's content is largely illegitimate and lacks detail and depth, exhibiting major deficiencies in the research base.
Organization	The project's organization is outstandingly logical, and the flow between ideas or sections is superbly smooth, demonstrating much forethought and preparation.	The project's organization is logical, with fluid transitions between most ideas or sections, demonstrating good preparation.	The project's organization is logical to some extent, but the flow between ideas or sections would benefit from stronger transitioning; overall, solid, but not exceptional preparation is evidenced.	The project's organization is largely illogical, and the flow between ideas or sections is awkward and/or jumpy in many places, demonstrating haphazard preparation.
Engagement of Audience/ Theatricality	The presentation to the audience is cleverly creative, highly original, and thoroughly engaging, exhibiting strong theatricality.	The presentation to the audience is creative, somewhat original, and engaging at many points, exhibiting present, but limited, theatricality.	The presentation to the audience is solid, but lacks creativity and originality at most points; the audience is engaged sporadically, but the presentation overall lacks theatricality.	The presentation to the audience is largely mundane or routine, greatly lacking originality; the audience's response is generally indifferent to the presentation's banality.
Adherence to Project Parameters	The presentation fits perfectly all of the assignment's parameters, such as time limit and/or included elements. *or* The presentation exceeds the assignment's parameters through the use of additional resources or elements.	The presentation fits most of the assignment's parameters, such as time limit and/or included elements.	The presentation fits only a limited amount of the assignment's parameters, such as time limit and/or included elements.	The presentation fits none of the assignment's parameters, such as time limit and/or included elements.

Total Score (out of 16 possible): _____

remember events, details, and facts largely because they hold personal meaning, because they relate somehow to the occurrences and details of people's emotional lives. Our favorite creative works, be they novels or movies or record albums, are just that, our *favorites*, in large part because of the personal significances that they hold for us, not because our instructors told us what *should* be our favorites. If we as educators want our lessons and our students' learning to stand the proverbial test of time, to stay with our pupils beyond the finite boundaries of classroom walls and school calendars, then we must allow them opportunities to personalize their learning.

I believe that in high school English classes nationwide, students are too often asked to recognize, absorb, and interpret the intentions, styles, and products of canonical authors and poets in a vacuous context, in terms concerned more with long-dead authors than with alive and well readers; too many students are never given opportunities to reflect upon or reframe those authors' and poets' visions and themes in relevant, personal ways. In my AP and pre-AP courses, I try to prod my students toward personal connections with literature by asking simplistic, albeit difficult to answer, questions such as "So what?", "Why should you care?", and "Why is this stuff relevant to your life?" Students who are able to answer these questions, no matter what work of literature is being considered, can find, digest, and personalize a work's humanness, to understand and truly *get* the true and lasting reasons why canonical artists and their work remain timelessly relevant.

Yes, it is educationally valid to utilize *The Scarlet Letter* as a mechanism for teaching generations of young people about Puritanism, appositive phrases, relative clauses, and the bureaucracy of 19th-century customs officers, but unless some theme, idea, conflict, or character in the play connects powerfully with an individual student somehow, then those arcane scholarly lessons will probably not long remain in the pupils' brains. Is not the point of reading literature at all—or studying anything, for that matter—to help you understand more clearly yourself, your life, and your world? Isn't that the reason why we chose to major in English, and in the cases of other teachers their own respective subjects, rather than something else? Personal connections with literature truly can be life-changing, as legions of literati can attest, and the provision to your students of an assignment to create individualized creative-interpretive projects aims to engender just those types of connections.

I have assigned such original products in my own AP classes for years, essentially as long as I have been teaching AP Literature, and the vast diversity of products that have been submitted over that time testifies to my students' amazing, entertaining, and too-often-untapped creative talents. One former student composed, utilizing a marimba and toms, a musical suite portraying *Hamlet*'s implication that knowledge and intelligence are a burdensome curse; another wrote, sang, and recorded a song concerning the abandonment of Frankenstein's monster, expressing how that betrayal mirrors her own felt experience as the daughter of divorcees. One year, someone related King Lear's obstinate hubris to modern athletics, designing and filming a mock sports report concerning the misguided blindness of arrogance and greed; others have painted and drawn thematic visualizations, skinned and tanned leather and molded wood for a Shakespearean dream catcher, designed and compiled photographic essays, twisted wire-hanger sculptures of dancing figures, and composed original narrative poems, short stories, or one-act plays. I've received shadow boxes, works of stained glass, mobiles and marionettes, stop-motion LEGO movies, computerized short films, monologues performed in class, paintings in oil and watercolor and everything in between, and interpretive dances! And, of all of the assignments that I require of my AP students, these creative-interpretive projects are by far the most enjoyable to grade; I look forward to them every year.

The assignment sheet on page 165 is one that you may distribute to your class if you wish to engage your own students in this intellectually stimulating and personally rewarding endeavor. Please emphasize when doing so the difference between creatively interpreting (i.e., reframing in an original way) aspects of *The Scarlet Letter* and, less creatively, regurgitating the plot or its characters in an alternative setting or situation. The former is the goal of this project, for personalized learning occurs when students are freed from the constraints of Hawthorne's original to focus instead on the truly human, universal heart of the story. Retelling the plot is one thing; truly understanding how its theme is relevant to your world is quite another!

As a mechanism for assessing the legitimacy of my students' creative thought processes as they relate to Hawthorne's novel, I ask them to submit short explanations of their artistic products (What is it? How did you make it?), their interpretive and creative goals in producing these original works (What were you shooting for? How does it relate to *The Scarlet Letter*?), and the degree to which they feel they succeeded in accomplishing their interpretive goals. Such explanation ensures that students submit original works that truly are relevant to the literature being studied, rather than off-the-cuff products taken from other unrelated classes, as well as articulate the relevancies of that literature to themselves.

I assess my students' creative-interpretive projects using the "numerical checklist" found on page 166, rather than with a traditional rubric delineating levels of success on traditional scholastic criteria. I feel that this flexible mechanism allows for a larger diversity of creative products, as the criteria outlined by this checklist are flexible enough that no matter what a student produces and submits, you can assess it using this instrument. Additionally, this checklist's emphasis on the holistic creation contrasts with the particular nature of most segmented rubrics, and in the assessment of creative products by students who are by and large probably not professional artists, but rather young learners trying out new ways of communicating, I personally prefer such a big-picture approach to assessment.

Conclusion

In teaching my own AP English Literature courses, I have utilized each of the six different approaches to writing outlined in this chapter. Not all at once, mind you, and perhaps not all in the same unit or even year of study, but all six of these compositional and reflective styles are appropriate and productive in preparation for success on the AP exam. If you do choose to utilize them in your own instruction, then I recommend their assignment to your students not in isolation, but rather overlapped as part of a larger reflective sequence: a research project spanning the unit . . . smaller AP and SAT-style essays as they proceed through the chapters . . . a longer analytical essay at the end . . . a creative-interpretive project to wrap it all up. Using a number of these assignments and evaluative devices will help you not only to improve your students' writing abilities wholesale, but also to develop their understanding, reflection upon, and retention of *The Scarlet Letter*'s importance and personal relevance beyond the scope of your individual unit of study.

Creative-Interpretive Project
The Scarlet Letter

In higher-level English classes nationwide, students are too often asked to reflect upon, interpret, and digest the artistic intentions of famous authors without being given the opportunity to reflect upon, interpret, and digest the importance of those authors' visions and themes as they relate to students' own lives. If you cannot relate a theme or philosophical concept to your world, then why bother to study it? Such an idea, an idea without personal utility, becomes inherently useless. In brief, the point of reading literature at all—or any idea, for that matter—is to help you better understand yourself, your own life, and your own world. I hope that this assignment provides you with an opportunity to do just that!

Requirements

- You are going to submit and reflect upon a creative interpretation—wholly of your own design—of one of *The Scarlet Letter*'s major themes.

- This interpretation can take any artistic shape that you wish: a self-made movie, narrative poem, one-act play, song (sung and/or played), series of related photographs, painting, interpretive dance, short story, symbolic marionette or collage, mock news broadcast, sculpture, or some amalgamation of many of the above.

- Your artistic piece does not need to mirror the story of *The Scarlet Letter* in any way, nor does it have to represent any of the literature's characters, settings, situations, etc. What it *must* do is represent in some tangible way one of the work's major *themes* (i.e., philosophical ideas such as the emotional difficulty of divided loyalties, the self-destructive nature of humans, the power of guilt, the futility of hiding secrets, etc.).

- Your creation is to be accompanied by a 400-to-600-word analysis, a self-reflection, upon both your creative work of art and the novel that influenced its creation, explaining just what theme(s) are portrayed in your own work, plus how and why they are important to you not just as a reader of literature, but also as a living, breathing, emotional human being.

Name: _____ Date: _____

Grading "Checklist" for Creative-Interpretive Project
The Scarlet Letter

Conceptual Validity
- The interpretive concept underlying the work of art is well thought-out, as explicated either by the work of art itself or by the accompanying analytical paper. _____/10
- It is clear, either upon viewing the work of art itself or after reading the accompanying paper, that at least one major theme of *The Scarlet Letter* is present and central to the concept of the newly created work of art. _____/10
- The artist's conceptualization of both this major theme and its representation in the new work of art is *not* contrary to Hawthorne's original conceptualization of the same theme, but parallel to it. _____/10

Accompanying Reflective Analysis
- The analytical paper that accompanies the work of art is between 400 and 600 words, and there are no major grammatical errors in it. _____/10
- The analytical paper reflects clearly and validly upon both the original work of literature and its inspirational effect upon the new work of art, explicating such important factors as their thematic bond, their philosophical views, and/or their sameness of mood. _____/10
- It is clear from the paper that the artist/student has thought about the original work of literature, its themes, and his or her own art not only thoroughly, but also well. _____/10

Overall Impression
- After viewing the work of art, I as the assessor feel that the artist/student has worked hard on this project, both intellectually and artistically. _____/20
- After viewing the work of art, I as the assessor am impressed both with the student's capacity for analyzing and reflecting upon philosophical, thematic literature and with his or her ability to correlate that literature with the "real world" of his or her life. _____/20

Total Score (Out of 100): _____

Chapter Materials

Name: _____ Date: _____

A → E → C Paragraph Practice for
"The Custom-House: Introductory to *The Scarlet Letter*"

Question: In this chapter, Nathaniel Hawthorne describes his discovery of a piece of antique cloth and an accompanying manuscript. Do you find his description of the circumstances surrounding this discovery to be more realistic or unrealistic? Why?

← Assertion/Topic Sentence

← Evidence From Chapter Supporting Assertion

← Commentary on Evidence

168 *The Scarlet Letter*

Name: _____ Date: _____

A → E → C Paragraph Practice for
The Scarlet Letter, Chapters 1–4

Question: In this series of chapters, we are introduced to Hester Prynne, her family, and her community. What is your impression of Hester based on these chapters, and to what other person or people might you compare her? Please support your answer with evidence and reason.

⬅ Assertion/Topic Sentence

⬅ Evidence From Chapter Supporting Assertion

⬅ Commentary on Evidence

Name: _____ Date: _____

A → E → C Paragraph Practice for
The Scarlet Letter, Chapters 5–6

Question: In these two chapters, we learn more about Hester Prynne's personal life and reaction to her required penance. What emotional or intellectual characteristics are here made evident to the reader, and how might they influence her response to Boston's punishment upon her? Please support your answer with evidence and reasoning.

⟵ Assertion/Topic Sentence

⟵ Evidence From Chapter Supporting Assertion

⟵ Commentary on Evidence

Name: _____ Date: _____

A → E → C Paragraph Practice for
The Scarlet Letter, Chapters 7–8

Question: In these two chapters, we observe interactions between Hester Prynne's daughter Pearl and prominent residents of Boston. Do you believe that Pearl's character is likely to aid her mother's social circumstances among their Bostonian neighbors or impair them? Please support your answer with evidence and reasoning.

← Assertion/Topic Sentence

← Evidence From Chapter Supporting Assertion

← Commentary on Evidence

Writing About The Scarlet Letter

Name: _____ Date: _____

A → E → C Paragraph Practice for
The Scarlet Letter, Chapters 9–11

Question: In this series of chapters, Roger Chillingworth's relationship with Arthur Dimmesdale is described. Based on the circumstances depicted, which of these two men is, in your opinion, the more upright ethically or morally, in other words, the more admirable? Please support your answer with evidence and reasoning.

← Assertion/Topic Sentence

← Evidence From Chapter Supporting Assertion

← Commentary on Evidence

Name: _____ Date: _____

A → E → C Paragraph Practice for
The Scarlet Letter, Chapters 12–15

Question: In these four chapters, Hawthorne exhibits dynamically evolving qualities of all four major characters: Hester Prynne, Pearl, Chillingworth, and Dimmesdale. Based on the depictions herein, which of these four characters do you believe to be the most greatly changed over the course of the novel so far? Please support your answer with evidence and reasoning.

⟵ Assertion/Topic Sentence

⟵ Evidence From Chapter Supporting Assertion

⟵ Commentary on Evidence

Writing About The Scarlet Letter

Name: _____ Date: _____

A → E → C Paragraph Practice for
The Scarlet Letter, Chapters 16–19

Question: In this set of chapters, Hawthorne utilizes symbolism to great effect in order to reinforce or otherwise emphasize his apparent themes. Which symbol or motif, as described within these four chapters, do you believe holds the most meaning relative to the major ideas of this novel so far? Please support your answer with evidence and reasoning.

← Assertion/Topic Sentence

← Evidence From Chapter Supporting Assertion

← Commentary on Evidence

Name: _____ Date: _____

A → E → C Paragraph Practice for
The Scarlet Letter, Chapters 20–23

Question: In these four chapters, Hawthorne's drama reaches its climax, and the townspeople of Boston coalesce just as the story's meaning does. At this conclusion of the novel's major plot, which character seems to you to be the most personally victorious, having accomplished by this point his or her goal most fully? Please support your answer with evidence and reasoning.

← Assertion/Topic Sentence

← Evidence From Chapter Supporting Assertion

← Commentary on Evidence

Name: _____ Date: _____

A → E → C Paragraph Practice for
The Scarlet Letter, Chapter 24

Question: In this final chapter of *The Scarlet Letter*, Hawthorne effectively describes the results of his emotional drama, creating a de facto epilogue. Based on the ends met and the outcomes encountered by the characters and society, do you believe that the conclusion of this novel is an appropriately fitting one? Please support your answer with evidence and reasoning.

← Assertion/Topic Sentence

← Evidence From Chapter Supporting Assertion

← Commentary on Evidence

Name: _____ Date: _____

AP-Style Essay Prompt
The Scarlet Letter, "The Custom-House"

Read carefully the following excerpt from "The Custom-House," the introductory chapter of *The Scarlet Letter*. Then compose a well-organized essay in which you analyze Hawthorne's emphasis on vision and appearance. Consider elements such as tone, diction, and symbolism. **Time limit: 40 minutes.**

The same torpor, as regarded the capacity for intellectual effort, accompanied me home, and weighed upon me in the chamber which I most absurdly termed my study. Nor did it quit me, when, late at night, I sat in the deserted parlor, lighted only
5 by the glimmering coal-fire and the moon, striving to picture forth imaginary scenes, which, the next day, might flow out on the brightening page in many-hued description.

If the imaginative faculty refused to act at such an hour, it might well be deemed a hopeless case. Moonlight, in a familiar
10 room, falling so white upon the carpet, and showing all its figures so distinctly,—making every object so minutely visible, yet so unlike a morning or noontide visibility,—is a medium the most suitable for a romance-writer to get acquainted with his illusive guests. There is the little domestic scenery of the well-
15 known apartment; the chairs, with each its separate individuality; the centre-table, sustaining a work-basket, a volume or two, and an extinguished lamp; the sofa; the book-case; the picture on the wall;—all these details, so completely seen, are so spiritualized by the unusual light, that they seem to lose their actual substance,
20 and become things of intellect. Nothing is too small or too trifling to undergo this change, and acquire dignity thereby. A child's shoe; the doll, seated in her little wicker carriage; the hobby-horse;—whatever, in a word, has been used or played with, during the day, is now invested with a quality of strangeness
25 and remoteness, though still almost as vividly present as by daylight. Thus, therefore, the floor of our familiar room has become a neutral territory, somewhere between the real world and fairy-land, where the Actual and the Imaginary may meet, and each imbue itself with the nature of the other. Ghosts
30 might enter here, without affrighting us. It would be too much in keeping with the scene to excite surprise, were we to look about us and discover a form, beloved, but gone hence, now sitting quietly in a streak of this magic moonshine, with an aspect that would make us doubt whether it had returned from
35 afar, or had never once stirred from our fireside.

The somewhat dim coal-fire has an essential influence in producing the effect which I would describe. It throws its unobtrusive tinge throughout the room, with a faint ruddiness upon the walls and ceiling, and a reflected gleam from the polish
40 of the furniture. This warmer light mingles itself with the cold spirituality of the moonbeams, and communicates, as it were, a heart and sensibilities of human tenderness to the forms which fancy summons up. It converts them from snow-images into men and women. Glancing at the looking-glass, we behold—
45 deep within its haunted verge—the smouldering glow of the half-extinguished anthracite, the white moonbeams on the floor, and a repetition of all the gleam and shadow of the picture, with one remove further from the actual, and nearer to the imaginative. Then, at such an hour, and with this scene before
50 him, if a man, sitting all alone, cannot dream strange things, and make them look like truth, he need never try to write romances.

Name: _____ Date: _____

AP-Style Essay Prompt
The Scarlet Letter, Chapters I–VI

Read carefully the following excerpt from the first six chapters of *The Scarlet Letter*. Then compose a well-organized essay in which you analyze Hawthorne's consideration of humans and the world of nature. Consider elements such as tone, diction, personification, and symbolism. **Time limit: 40 minutes.**

    A throng of bearded men, in sad-colored garments, and gray, steeple-crowned hats, intermixed with women, some wearing hoods, and others bareheaded, was assembled in front of a wooden edifice, the door of which was heavily timbered
5 with oak, and studded with iron spikes.
    The founders of a new colony, whatever Utopia of human virtue and happiness they might originally project, have invariably recognized it among their earliest practical necessities to allot a portion of the virgin soil as a cemetery, and another portion
10 as the site of a prison. In accordance with this rule, it may safely be assumed that the forefathers of Boston had built the first prison-house somewhere in the vicinity of Cornhill, almost as seasonably as they marked out the first burial-ground, on Isaac Johnson's lot, and round about his grave, which
15 subsequently became the nucleus of all the congregated sepulchres in the old church-yard of King's Chapel. Certain it is, that, some fifteen or twenty years after the settlement of the town, the wooden jail was already marked with weather-stains and other indications of age, which gave a yet darker aspect to its
20 beetle-browed and gloomy front. The rust on the ponderous iron-work of its oaken door looked more antique than anything else in the New World. Like all that pertains to crime, it seemed never to have known a youthful era. Before this ugly edifice, and between it and the wheel-track of the street, was a grass-plot,
25 much overgrown with burdock, pig-weed, apple-peru, and such unsightly vegetation, which evidently found something congenial in the soil that had so early borne the black flower of civilized society, a prison. But, on one side of the portal, and rooted almost at the threshold, was a wild rose-bush, covered, in this
30 month of June, with its delicate gems, which might be imagined to offer their fragrance and fragile beauty to the prisoner as he went in, and to the condemned criminal as he came forth to his doom, in token that the deep heart of Nature could pity and be kind to him.
35   This rose-bush, by a strange chance, has been kept alive in history; but whether it had merely survived out of the stern old wilderness, so long after the fall of the gigantic pines and oaks that originally overshadowed it,—or whether, as there is fair authority for believing, it had sprung up under the footsteps
40 of the sainted Ann Hutchinson, as she entered the prison door,—we shall not take upon us to determine. Finding it so directly on the threshold of our narrative, which is now about to issue from that inauspicious portal, we could hardly do otherwise than pluck one of its flowers, and present it to the
45 reader. It may serve, let us hope, to symbolize some sweet moral blossom, that may be found along the track, or relieve the darkening close of a tale of human frailty and sorrow.

Name: _____ Date: _____

AP-Style Essay Prompt
The Scarlet Letter, Chapters VII–XII

Read carefully the following excerpt from Chapters 7–12 of *The Scarlet Letter*. Then compose a well-organized essay in which you analyze this selection's particular atmosphere. Consider elements such as tone, implication, symbolism, and irony. **Time limit: 40 minutes.**

One day, leaning his forehead on his hand, and his elbow on the sill of the open window, that looked towards the grave-yard, [Mr. Dimmesdale] talked with Roger Chillingworth, while the old man was examining a bundle of unsightly plants.

5 "Where," asked he, with a look askance at them,—for it was the clergyman's peculiarity that he seldom, now-a-days, looked straight-forth at any object, whether human or inanimate—"where, my kind doctor, did you gather those herbs, with such a dark, flabby leaf?"

10 "Even in the grave-yard here at hand," answered the physician, continuing his employment. "They are new to me. I found them growing on a grave, which bore no tomb-stone, nor other memorial of the dead man, save these ugly weeds, that have taken upon themselves to keep him in remembrance. They grew
15 out of his heart, and typify, it may be, some hideous secret that was buried with him, and which he had done better to confess during his lifetime."

"Perchance," said Mr. Dimmesdale, "he earnestly desired it, but could not."

20 "And wherefore?" rejoined the physician. "Wherefore not; since all the powers of nature call so earnestly for the confession of sin, that these black weeds have sprung up out of a buried heart, to make manifest an unspoken crime?"

"That, good Sir, is but a fantasy of yours," replied the
25 minister. "There can be, if I forebode aright, no power, short of the Divine mercy, to disclose, whether by uttered words, or by type or emblem, the secrets that may be buried with a human heart. The heart, making itself guilty of such secrets, must perforce hold them, until the day when all hidden things shall
30 be revealed. Nor have I so read or interpreted Holy Writ, as to understand that the disclosure of human thoughts and deeds, then to be made, is intended as a part of the retribution. That, surely, were a shallow view of it. No; these revelations, unless I greatly err, are meant merely to promote the intellectual
35 satisfaction of all intelligent beings, who will stand waiting, on that day, to see the dark problem of this life made plain. A knowledge of men's hearts will be needful to the completest solution of that problem. And I conceive, moreover, that the hearts holding such miserable secrets as you speak of will
40 yield them up, at that last day, not with reluctance, but with a joy unutterable."

"Then why not reveal them here?" asked Roger Chillingworth, glancing quietly aside at the minister. "Why should not the guilty ones sooner avail themselves of this unutterable solace?"

45 "They mostly do," said the clergyman, griping hard at his breast, as if afflicted with an importunate throb of pain. "Many, many a poor soul hath given its confidence to me, not only on the death-bed, but while strong in life, and fair in reputation. And ever, after such an outpouring, O, what a relief have I witnessed
50 in those sinful brethren! even as in one who at last draws free air, after long stifling with his own polluted breath. How can it be otherwise? Why should a wretched man, guilty, we will say, of murder, prefer to keep the dead corpse buried in his own heart, rather than fling it forth at once, and let the universe take
55 care of it!"

"Yet some men bury their secrets thus," observed the calm physician.

"True; there are such men," answered Mr. Dimmesdale.

Name: _____ Date: _____

AP-Style Essay Prompt
The Scarlet Letter, Chapters XIII–XVIII

Read carefully the two excerpts found below, both taken from Chapters 13–18 of *The Scarlet Letter*. Then compose a well-organized essay in which you compare and contrast the two selection's portrayals of nature. Consider such elements as diction, tone, and figurative language. **Time limit: 40 minutes.**

Excerpt 1

"Is the world, then, so narrow?" exclaimed Hester Prynne, fixing her deep eyes on the minister's, and instinctively exercising a magnetic power over a spirit so shattered and subdued that it could hardly hold itself erect. "Doth the universe lie within the compass of yonder town, which only a little time ago was but a leaf-strewn desert, as lonely as this around us? Whither leads yonder forest track? Backward to the settlement, thou sayest! Yes; but onward, too! Deeper it goes, and deeper, into the wilderness, less plainly to be seen at every step; until, some few miles hence, the yellow leaves will show no vestige of the white man's tread. There thou art free! So brief a journey would bring thee from a world where thou hast been most wretched, to one where thou mayest still be happy! Is there not shade enough in all this boundless forest to hide thy heart from the gaze of Roger Chillingworth?"

"Yes, Hester; but only under the fallen leaves!" replied the minister, with a sad smile.

"Then there is the broad pathway of the sea!" continued Hester. "It brought thee hither. If thou so choose, it will bear the back again. In our native land, whether in some remote rural village or in vast London,—or, surely, in Germany, in France, in pleasant Italy,—thou wouldst be beyond his power and knowledge! And what hast thou to do with all these iron me, and their opinions? They have kept thy better part in bondage too long already!"

Excerpt 2

So speaking, she undid the clasp that fastened the scarlet letter, and, taking it from her bosom, threw it to a distance among the withered leaves. The mystic token alighted on the hither verge of the stream. With a hand's breadth further flight it would have fallen into the water, and have given the little brook another woe to carry onward, besides the unintelligible tale which it still kept murmuring about. But there lay the embroidered letter, glittering like a lost jewel, which some ill-fated wanderer might pick up, and thenceforth be haunted by strange phantoms of guilt, sinkings of the heart, and unaccountable misfortune.

The stigma gone, Hester heaved a long, deep sigh, in which the burden of shame and anguish departed from her spirit. O exquisite relief! She had not known the weight, until she felt the freedom! By another impulse, she took off the formal cap that confined her hair; and down it fell upon her shoulders, dark and rich, with at once a shadow and a light in its abundance, and imparting the charm of softness to her features. There played around her mouth, and beamed out of her eyes, a radiant and tender smile, that seemed gushing from the very heart of womanhood. A crimson flush was glowing on her cheek, that had been long so pale. Her sex, her youth, and the whole richness of her beauty, came back from what men call the irrevocable past, and clustered themselves, with her maiden hope, and a happiness before unknown, within the magic circle of this hour. And, as if the gloom of the earth and sky had been but the effluence of these two mortal hearts, it vanished with their sorrow. All at once, as with a sudden smile of heaven, forth burst the sunshine, pouring a very flood into the obscure forest, gladdening each green leaf, transmuting the yellow fallen ones to gold, that had made a shadow hitherto, embodied the brightness now. The course of the little brook might be traced by its merry gleam afar into the wood's heart of mystery, which had become a mystery of joy.

Such was the sympathy of Nature—that wild, heathen Nature of the forest, never subjugated by human law, nor illumined by higher truth—with the bliss of these two spirits! Love, whether newly born or aroused from a death-like slumber, must always create a sunshine, filling the heart so full of radiance, that it overflows upon the outward world.

Name: _____ Date: _____

AP-Style Essay Prompt
The Scarlet Letter, Chapters XIX–XXIV

Read carefully the following excerpt from the final six chapters of *The Scarlet Letter*. Then compose a well-organized essay in which you analyze the effects of the narrator's choices in diction and syntax. Consider elements such as tone, punctuation, euphony, and assonant and consonant devices. **Time limit: 40 minutes.**

By this time the preliminary prayer had been offered in the meeting-house, and the accents of the Reverend Mr. Dimmesdale were heard commencing his discourse. An irresistible feeling kept Hester near the spot. As the sacred edifice was too
5 much thronged to admit another auditor, she took up her position close beside the scaffold of the pillory. It was in sufficient proximity to bring the whole sermon to her ears, in the shape of an indistinct, but varied, murmur and flow of the minister's very peculiar voice.
10   This vocal organ was in itself a rich endowment; insomuch that a listener, comprehending nothing of the language in which the preacher spoke, might still have been swayed to and fro by the mere tone and cadence. Like all other music, it breathed passion and pathos, and emotions high or tender, in a
15 tongue native to the human heart, wherever educated. Muffled as the sound was by its passage through the church-walls, Hester Prynne listened with such intentness, and sympathized so intimately, that the sermon had throughout a meaning for her, entirely apart from its indistinguishable words. These, perhaps,
20 if more distinctly heard, might have been only a grosser medium, and have clogged the spiritual sense. Now she caught the low undertone, as of the wind sinking down to repose itself; then ascended with it, as it rose through progressive gradations of sweetness and power, until its volume seemed to envelop her
25 with an atmosphere of awe and solemn grandeur. And yet, majestic as the voice sometimes became, there was forever in it an essential character of plaintiveness. A loud or low expression of anguish,—the whisper, or the shriek, as it might be conceived, of suffering humanity, that touched a sensibility in every
30 bosom! At times this deep strain of pathos was all that could be heard, and scarcely heard, sighing amid a desolate silence. But even when the minister's voice grew high and commanding,—when it gushed irrepressibly upward,—when it assumed its utmost breadth and power, so overfilling the church as to burst
35 its way through the solid walls, and diffuse itself in the open air,—still, if the auditor listened intently, and for the purpose, he could detect the same cry of pain. What was it? The complaint of a human heart, sorrow-laden, perchance guilty, telling its secret, whether of guilt or sorrow, to the great heart
40 of mankind; beseeching its sympathy or forgiveness,—at every moment,—in each accent,—and never in vain! It was this profound and continual undertone that gave the clergyman his most appropriate power.

Resources for Further Study

Abel, D. (1988). *The moral picturesque: Studies in Hawthorne's fiction*. West Lafayette, IN: Purdue University Press.

Alvis, J. E. (2012). *Nathaniel Hawthorne as political philosopher: Revolutionary principles domesticated and personalized*. New Brunswick, NJ: Transaction Publishers.

Barlowe, J. (2000). *The scarlet mob of scribblers: Rereading Hester Prynne*. Carbondale, IL: Southern Illinois University Press.

Baym, N. (1986). The Scarlet Letter: *A reading*. Boston, MA: Twayne Publishers.

Bell, M. (1962). *Hawthorne's view of the artist*. New York, NY: State University of New York Press.

Bell, M. (Ed., 1993). *New essays on Hawthorne's major tales*. New York, NY: Cambridge University Press.

Bercovitch, S. (1992). *The office of* The Scarlet Letter. Baltimore, MD: Johns Hopkins University Press.

Bird, O., & Bird, K. (2004). *From witchery to sanctity: The religious vicissitudes of the Hawthornes*. South Bend, IN: St. Augustine's Press.

Bloom, H. (Ed.). (2007). *Modern critical interpretations: Nathaniel Hawthorne's* The Scarlet Letter (2nd ed.). New York, NY: Chelsea House Publishers.

Boewe, C., & Murphy, M. G. (1960). Hester Prynne in history. *American Literature, 32*, 202–204.

Brodhead, R. H. (1990). *The school of Hawthorne*. New York, NY: Oxford University Press.

Canaris, V., & von Mengershausen, J. (Producers), & Wenders, W. (Director). (1973). *The scarlet letter* [Motion picture]. West Germany: Elías Querejeta Producciones Cinematográficas S.L.

Center for Gifted Education. (1998). *Guide to teaching a language arts curriculum for high ability learners*. Dubuque, IA: Kendall/Hunt.

Chase, R. V. (1980). Hawthorne and the limits of romance. In *The American novel and its traditions*. Baltimore, MD: Johns Hopkins University Press.

Coale, S. C. (2011). *The entanglements of Nathaniel Hawthorne: Haunted minds and ambiguous approaches*. Rochester, NY: Camden House.

Colacurcio, M. J. (Ed.). (1985). *New essays on* The Scarlet Letter. New York, NY: Cambridge University Press.

Cottom, D. (1981). Hawthorne versus Hester: The ghostly dialectic of romance in *The Scarlet Letter*. *Texas Studies in Literature and Language, 24,* 47–67.

Crews, F. C. (1966). *The sins of the fathers: Hawthorne's psychological themes*. New York, NY: Oxford University Press.

Darmour, L. (Producer), & Vignola, R.G. (Director). (1934). *The scarlet letter* [Motion picture]. United States: Larry Darmour Productions.

Dauber, K. (1977). *Rediscovering Hawthorne*. Princeton, NJ: Princeton University Press.

Davis, G. A., Rimm, S. B., & Siegle, D. (2010). *Education of the gifted and talented* (6th ed.). New York, NY: Pearson.

Demos, J. P. (2004). *Entertaining Satan: Witchcraft and the culture of early New England* (Updated ed.). New York, NY: Oxford University Press.

Devine, Z., & Gluck, W. (Producers), & Gluck, W. (Director). (2010). *Easy a* [Motion picture]. United States: Screen Gems.

Dunne, M. (1995). *Hawthorne's narrative strategies*. Jackson: University Press of Mississippi.

Egan, K. (1995). The adultress in the market-place: Hawthorne and *The Scarlet Letter*. *Studies in the Novel, 27,* 26–41.

Fogle, R. H. (1964). *Hawthorne's fiction: The light and the dark*. Norman, OK: University of Oklahoma Press.

Gale, R. L. (1991). *A Nathaniel Hawthorne encyclopedia*. New York, NY: Greenwood Press.

Gilmore, M. T. (1988). *American Romanticism and the marketplace*. Chicago, IL: University of Chicago Press.

Green, C. (1980). "The Custom-House": Hawthorne's dark wood of error. *New England Quarterly, 53,* 184–195.

Hauser, R., & Hirschman, H. (Producers), & Hauser, R. (Director). (1979). *The scarlet letter* [Televised miniseries]. United States: WGBH.

Herbert, T. W. (1995). *Dearest beloved: The Hawthornes and the making of the middle-class family*. Berkeley, CA: University of California Press.

Idol, J. L., Jr., & Ponder, M. (Eds.). (1999). *Hawthorne and women: Engendering and expanding the Hawthorne tradition.* Amherst, MA: University of Massachusetts Press.

Joffé, R., & Vajna, A. G. (Producers), & Joffé, R. (Director). (1995). *The scarlet letter* [Motion picture]. United States: Mill Creek.

Jordan, H. (2011). *When she woke.* Chapel Hill, NC: Algonquin Books of Chapel Hill.

Kaul, A. N. (Ed.). (1966). *Hawthorne: A collection of critical essays.* Englewood Cliffs, NJ: Prentice-Hall.

Kennedy-Andrews, E. (Ed.). (2000). *Columbia critical guides Nathaniel Hawthorne*: The Scarlet Letter. New York, NY: Columbia University Press.

Kesterson, D. B. (Ed.). (1988). *Critical essays on Hawthorne's* The Scarlet Letter. Boston, MA: G. K. Hall.

Kopley, R. (2003). *The threads of* The Scarlet Letter: *A study of Hawthorne's transformative art.* Newark, DE: University of Delaware Press.

Laemmle, C. (Producer), & Smiley, J. W., & Tucker, G.L. (Directors). (1911). *The scarlet letter* [Motion picture]. United States: Independent Moving Pictures Co. of America (IMP).

Lathrop, G. P. (Librettist), & Damrosch, W. (Composer). (1896). *The scarlet letter: A dramatic composition.* Washington, DC: The Library of Congress.

Lawrence, D. H. (1977). *Studies in classic American literature.* New York, NY: Penguin Books. (Original work published 1923).

Levin, H. (1960). *The power of blackness: Hawthorne, Melville, Poe.* New York, NY: Vintage Books.

Loving, J. (1993). Hawthorne's awakening in the customhouse. In *Lost in the customhouse: Authorship in the American Renaissance* (pp. 19–34). Iowa City: University of Iowa Press.

Madsen, D. L. (1991). 'A for abolition': Hawthorne's bond-servant and the shadow of slavery. *Journal of American Studies, 25,* 255–259.

Mason, D. (2012). *The scarlet libretto.* Pasadena, CA: Red Hen Press.

Mellow, J. R. (1998). *Nathaniel Hawthorne in his times.* Baltimore, MD: Johns Hopkins University Press.

Miller, E. H. (1992). *Salem is my dwelling place: a life of Nathaniel Hawthorne.* Iowa City, IA: University of Iowa Press.

Miller, J. H. (1991). *Hawthorne and history: Defacing it.* Cambridge, UK: Basil Blackwell.

Moers, E. (1985). *The Scarlet Letter*: A political reading. *Prospects, 9,* 49–70.

Moore, M. (2001). *The Salem world of Nathaniel Hawthorne.* Columbia: University of Missouri Press.

Mukherjee, B. (1993). *The holder of the world.* New York, NY: Fawcett Books.

Parks, S. L. (1999). *In the blood.* New York, NY: Dramatists Play Service, Inc.

Paul, R. (1993). *Critical thinking: What every person needs to survive in a rapidly changing world*. Rohnert Park, CA: Foundation for Critical Thinking.

Pearce, R. H. (Ed.). (1964). *Hawthorne centenary essays*. Columbus, OH: Ohio State University Press.

Pimple, K. D. (1993). "Subtle, but remorseful hypocrite": Dimmesdale's moral character. *Studies in the Novel, 25,* 257–271.

Reynolds, L. J. (Ed.). (2001). *A historical guide to Nathaniel Hawthorne*. New York, NY: Oxford University Press.

Reynolds, L. J. (2010). *Devils and rebels: The making of Hawthorne's damned politics*. Ann Arbor: The University of Michigan Press.

Schiff, J. (1992). *Updike's version: Rewriting* The Scarlet Letter. Columbia: University of Missouri Press.

Small, M. (1980). Hawthorne's *The Scarlet Letter*: Arthur Dimmesdale's manipulation of language. *American Imago, 37,* 113–123.

Stearns, F. P. (1906). *The life and genius of Nathaniel Hawthorne*. Philadelphia, PA: J. B. Lippincott Company.

Stein, W. B. (1953). *Hawthorne's Faust: A study of the devil archetype*. Gainesville, FL: University of Florida Press.

Swann, C. (2009). *Nathaniel Hawthorne: Tradition and revolution*. New York, NY: Oxford University Press.

Taylor, J. G. (1965). *Hawthorne's ambivalence toward Puritanism*. Logan, UT: Utah State University Press.

Tomc, S. (2002). A change of heart: Hester, Hawthorne, and the service of love. *Nineteenth-Century Literature, 56,* 466–494.

Updike, J. (1986). *Roger's version*. New York, NY: Alfred A. Knopf.

Van Doren, M. (1949). *Nathaniel Hawthorne*. New York, NY: William Sloane Associates.

Waggoneer, H. H. (1963). *Hawthorne: A critical study* (Rev ed.). Cambridge, MA: Harvard University Press.

References

Bradstreet, A. (2007a). The author to her book. In G. Perkins & B. Perkins (Eds.), *The American tradition in literature* (11th ed.; p. 76). New York, NY: McGraw Hill. (Original work published 1678)

Bradstreet, A. (2007b). To my dear and loving husband. In G. Perkins & B. Perkins (Eds.), *The American tradition in literature* (11th ed.; p. 77). New York, NY: McGraw Hill. (Original work published 1678)

Center for Gifted Education. (2011). *Change through choices: A language arts unit for high-ability learners* (2nd ed.). Dubuque, IA: Kendall Hunt Publishing Company.

College Board: Advanced Placement Program. (2007). *English language and composition, English literature and composition: Course description.* Princeton, NJ: Author. Retrieved from http://apcentral.collegeboard.com/apc/public/repository/52272_apenglocked5_30_4309.pdf

Common Core State Standards Initiative. (2012). *English language arts standards.* Retrieved from http://www.corestandards.org/ELA-Literacy

Edwards, J. (2007). Sarah Pierrepont. In G. Perkins & B. Perkins (Eds.), *The American tradition in literature* (11th ed.; pp. 161–162). New York, NY: McGraw Hill. (Original work written circa 1723)

Emerson, R. W. (2007). Nature. In G. Perkins & B. Perkins (Eds.), *The American tradition in literature* (11th ed.; pp. 368–395). New York, NY: McGraw Hill. (Original work published 1836)

Giouroukakis, V., & Connolly, M. (2012). *Getting to the core of English language arts, grades 6–12; How to meet the Common Core State Standards with lessons from the classroom.* Thousand Oaks, CA: Corwin.

Golding, W. (2006). *Lord of the flies*. New York, NY: Penguin. (Original work published 1954)

Hawthorne, N. (2005). *The scarlet letter and other writings* (L. S. Person, Ed.). New York, NY: W.W. Norton & Company. (Original work published 1850)

Jago, C. (2011). *With rigor for all: Meeting Common Core Standards for reading literature* (2nd ed.). Portsmouth, NH: Heinemann.

Jefferson, T. (2007). The declaration of independence. In G. Perkins & B. Perkins (Eds.), *The American tradition in literature* (11th ed.; pp. 259–262). New York, NY: McGraw Hill. (Original work written 1776)

National Council of Teachers of English, & International Reading Association. (1996). *Standards of learning for the English language arts*. Urbana, IL: Author.

Sigourney, L. H. H. (2007). The Indian's welcome to the Pilgrim fathers. In G. Perkins & B. Perkins (Eds.), *The American tradition in literature* (11th ed.; pp. 623–624). New York, NY: McGraw Hill. (Original work published 1835)

Silver, H. F., Dewing, R. T., & Perini, M. J. (2012). *The core six: Essential strategies for achieving excellence with the Common Core*. Alexandria, VA: ASCD.

VanTassel-Baska, J. (1986). Effective curriculum and instructional models for the gifted. *Gifted Child Quarterly, 30,* 164–169.

Wheatley, P. (2007). On being brought from Africa to America. In G. Perkins & B. Perkins (Eds.), *The American tradition in literature* (11th ed.; p. 283). New York, NY: McGraw Hill. (Original work published 1773)

About the Author

R. Brigham Lampert, dual-certified in English and Gifted Education, is among a small and select group of professional educators named by the Virginia Department of Education as an endorsed Teacher as Leader. Also a National Board Certified Teacher in English Language Arts, Lampert has been nominated for several national commendations, including a 2008 Nobel Educator of Distinction selection by the National Society of High School Scholars and a 2006 Disney Teacher Award. He has studied and worked extensively at the College of William and Mary, where he was awarded a scholarship for Excellence in Gifted Education and earned his M.Ed., and he received his bachelor's degree in English from Haverford College.

Lampert has additionally authored *Advanced Placement Classroom: King Lear*, *Advanced Placement Classroom: Romeo and Juliet,* and *Perfect 800: SAT Verbal*, all available from Prufrock Press, original poems in various national journals, and six Shakespearean titles in the College of William and Mary's Center for Gifted Education's *Navigator* series, as well as coauthored and edited three updated editions of the Center's award-winning literature units for gifted learners. Additionally trained as a building administrator, Lampert chairs the English department at Jamestown High School in Williamsburg, VA, where he and his family reside.

Common Core State Standards Alignment

Grade Level	Common Core State Standards
Grade 7 ELA-Literacy	RL.7.1 Cite several pieces of textual evidence to support analysis of what the text says explicitly as well as inferences drawn from the text.
	RL.7.2 Determine a theme or central idea of a text and analyze its development over the course of the text; provide an objective summary of the text.
	RL.7.3 Analyze how particular elements of a story or drama interact (e.g., how setting shapes the characters or plot).
	RL.7.4 Determine the meaning of words and phrases as they are used in a text, including figurative and connotative meanings; analyze the impact of rhymes and other repetitions of sounds (e.g., alliteration) on a specific verse or stanza of a poem or section of a story or drama.
	RL.7.5 Analyze how a drama's or poem's form or structure (e.g., soliloquy, sonnet) contributes to its meaning
	RL.7.6 Analyze how an author develops and contrasts the points of view of different characters or narrators in a text.
	RL.7.7 Compare and contrast a written story, drama, or poem to its audio, filmed, staged, or multimedia version, analyzing the effects of techniques unique to each medium (e.g., lighting, sound, color, or camera focus and angles in a film).
	W.7.2 Write informative/explanatory texts to examine a topic and convey ideas, concepts, and information through the selection, organization, and analysis of relevant content.
	W.7.9 Draw evidence from literary or informational texts to support analysis, reflection, and research.

Grade Level	Common Core State Standards
Grade 7 ELA-Literacy, *continued*	SL.7.1 Engage effectively in a range of collaborative discussions (one-on-one, in groups, and teacher-led) with diverse partners on grade 7 topics, texts, and issues, building on others' ideas and expressing their own clearly.
	SL.7.4 Present claims and findings, emphasizing salient points in a focused, coherent manner with pertinent descriptions, facts, details, and examples; use appropriate eye contact, adequate volume, and clear pronunciation.
	L.7.5 Demonstrate understanding of figurative language, word relationships, and nuances in word meanings.
Grade 8 ELA-Literacy	RL.8.1 Cite the textual evidence that most strongly supports an analysis of what the text says explicitly as well as inferences drawn from the text.
	RL.8.2 Determine a theme or central idea of a text and analyze its development over the course of the text, including its relationship to the characters, setting, and plot; provide an objective summary of the text.
	RL.8.3 Analyze how particular lines of dialogue or incidents in a story or drama propel the action, reveal aspects of a character, or provoke a decision.
	RL.8.4 Determine the meaning of words and phrases as they are used in a text, including figurative and connotative meanings; analyze the impact of specific word choices on meaning and tone, including analogies or allusions to other texts.
	RL.8.6 Analyze how differences in the points of view of the characters and the audience or reader (e.g., created through the use of dramatic irony) create such effects as suspense or humor.
	RL.8.7 Analyze the extent to which a filmed or live production of a story or drama stays faithful to or departs from the text or script, evaluating the choices made by the director or actors.
	W.8.2 Write informative/explanatory texts to examine a topic and convey ideas, concepts, and information through the selection, organization, and analysis of relevant content.
	W.8.9 Draw evidence from literary or informational texts to support analysis, reflection, and research.
	SL.8.1 Engage effectively in a range of collaborative discussions (one-on-one, in groups, and teacher-led) with diverse partners on grade 8 topics, texts, and issues, building on others' ideas and expressing their own clearly.
	SL.8.4 Present claims and findings, emphasizing salient points in a focused, coherent manner with relevant evidence, sound valid reasoning, and well-chosen details; use appropriate eye contact, adequate volume, and clear pronunciation.
	L.8.5 Demonstrate understanding of figurative language, word relationships, and nuances in word meanings.

Grade Level	Common Core State Standards
Grade 9-10 ELA-Literacy	RL.9-10.1 Cite strong and thorough textual evidence to support analysis of what the text says explicitly as well as inferences drawn from the text.
	RL.9-10.2 Determine a theme or central idea of a text and analyze in detail its development over the course of the text, including how it emerges and is shaped and refined by specific details; provide an objective summary of the text.
	RL.9-10.3 Analyze how complex characters (e.g., those with multiple or conflicting motivations) develop over the course of a text, interact with other characters, and advance the plot or develop the theme.
	RL.9-10.4 Determine the meaning of words and phrases as they are used in the text, including figurative and connotative meanings; analyze the cumulative impact of specific word choices on meaning and tone (e.g., how the language evokes a sense of time and place; how it sets a formal or informal tone).
	RL.9-10.5 Analyze how an author's choices concerning how to structure a text, order events within it (e.g., parallel plots), and manipulate time (e.g., pacing, flashbacks) create such effects as mystery, tension, or surprise.
	RL.9-10.9 Analyze how an author draws on and transforms source material in a specific work (e.g., how Shakespeare treats a theme or topic from Ovid or the Bible or how a later author draws on a play by Shakespeare).
	W.9-10.2 Write informative/explanatory texts to examine and convey complex ideas, concepts, and information clearly and accurately through the effective selection, organization, and analysis of content.
	W.9-10.9 Draw evidence from literary or informational texts to support analysis, reflection, and research.
	W.9-10.10 Write routinely over extended time frames (time for research, reflection, and revision) and shorter time frames (a single sitting or a day or two) for a range of tasks, purposes, and audiences.
	SL.9-10.1 Initiate and participate effectively in a range of collaborative discussions (one-on-one, in groups, and teacher-led) with diverse partners on grades 9–10 topics, texts, and issues, building on others' ideas and expressing their own clearly and persuasively.
	SL.9-10.6 Adapt speech to a variety of contexts and tasks, demonstrating command of formal English when indicated or appropriate. (See grades 9–10 Language standards 1 and 3 here for specific expectations.)
	L.9-10.5 Demonstrate understanding of figurative language, word relationships, and nuances in word meanings.

Grade Level	Common Core State Standards
Grade 9-10 ELA-Literacy, *continued*	L.9-10.6 Acquire and use accurately general academic and domain-specific words and phrases, sufficient for reading, writing, speaking, and listening at the college and career readiness level; demonstrate independence in gathering vocabulary knowledge when considering a word or phrase important to comprehension or expression.
Grade 11-12 ELA-Literacy	RL.11-12.1 Cite strong and thorough textual evidence to support analysis of what the text says explicitly as well as inferences drawn from the text, including determining where the text leaves matters uncertain.
	RL.11-12.2 Determine two or more themes or central ideas of a text and analyze their development over the course of the text, including how they interact and build on one another to produce a complex account; provide an objective summary of the text.
	RL.11-12.3 Analyze the impact of the author's choices regarding how to develop and relate elements of a story or drama (e.g., where a story is set, how the action is ordered, how the characters are introduced and developed).
	RL.11-12.4 Determine the meaning of words and phrases as they are used in the text, including figurative and connotative meanings; analyze the impact of specific word choices on meaning and tone, including words with multiple meanings or language that is particularly fresh, engaging, or beautiful. (Include Shakespeare as well as other authors.)
	RL.11-12.5 Analyze how an author's choices concerning how to structure specific parts of a text (e.g., the choice of where to begin or end a story, the choice to provide a comedic or tragic resolution) contribute to its overall structure and meaning as well as its aesthetic impact.
	RL.11-12.6 Analyze a case in which grasping a point of view requires distinguishing what is directly stated in a text from what is really meant (e.g., satire, sarcasm, irony, or understatement).
	RL.11-12.7 Analyze multiple interpretations of a story, drama, or poem (e.g., recorded or live production of a play or recorded novel or poetry), evaluating how each version interprets the source text. (Include at least one play by Shakespeare and one play by an American dramatist.)
	RL.11-12.9 Demonstrate knowledge of eighteenth-, nineteenth- and early-twentieth-century foundational works of American literature, including how two or more texts from the same period treat similar themes or topics.

Grade Level	Common Core State Standards
Grade 11-12 ELA-Literacy, *continued*	RL.11-12.10 By the end of grade 11, read and comprehend literature, including stories, dramas, and poems, in the grades 11-CCR text complexity band proficiently, with scaffolding as needed at the high end of the range. By the end of grade 12, read and comprehend literature, including stories, dramas, and poems, at the high end of the grades 11-CCR text complexity band independently and proficiently.
	W.11-12.2 Write informative/explanatory texts to examine and convey complex ideas, concepts, and information clearly and accurately through the effective selection, organization, and analysis of content.
	W.11-12.9 Draw evidence from literary or informational texts to support analysis, reflection, and research.
	W.11-12.10 Write routinely over extended time frames (time for research, reflection, and revision) and shorter time frames (a single sitting or a day or two) for a range of tasks, purposes, and audiences.
	SL.11-12.1 Initiate and participate effectively in a range of collaborative discussions (one-on-one, in groups, and teacher-led) with diverse partners on grades 11–12 topics, texts, and issues, building on others' ideas and expressing their own clearly and persuasively.
	SL.11-12.6 Adapt speech to a variety of contexts and tasks, demonstrating a command of formal English when indicated or appropriate. (See grades 11–12 Language standards 1 and 3 here for specific expectations.)
	L.11-12.5 Demonstrate understanding of figurative language, word relationships, and nuances in word meanings.
	L.11-12.6 Acquire and use accurately general academic and domain-specific words and phrases, sufficient for reading, writing, speaking, and listening at the college and career readiness level; demonstrate independence in gathering vocabulary knowledge when considering a word or phrase important to comprehension or expression.

For Product Safety Concerns and Information please contact our EU representative GPSR@taylorandfrancis.com
Taylor & Francis Verlag GmbH, Kaufingerstraße 24, 80331 München, Germany

www.ingramcontent.com/pod-product-compliance
Lightning Source LLC
Chambersburg PA
CBHW080410300426
44113CB00015B/2468